AGING
IN CANADIAN
S O C I E T Y

a survey

AGING
IN CANADIAN
S O C I E T Y

a survey

Maureen Baker, Ph.D.
Research Branch
Library of Parliament
Ottawa

McGRAW-HILL RYERSON LIMITED

Toronto   Montreal   New York   Auckland
Bogotá   Cairo   Caracas   Hamburg   Lisbon
London   Madrid   Mexico   Milan   New Delhi
Panama   Paris   San Juan   São Paulo
Singapore   Sydney   Tokyo

AGING IN CANADIAN SOCIETY: *a survey*

ISBN 0-07-549173-7

1234567890   M   7654321098

Printed and bound in Canada

Care has been taken to trace ownership of copyright material contained in this text. The publishers will gladly take any information that will enable them to rectify any reference or credit in subsequent editions.

Canadian Cataloguing in Publication Data

Baker, Maureen
  Aging in Canadian society

Bibliography: p.
Includes index.
ISBN 0-07-549173-7

1. Aged — Canada.   2. Aged — Canada — Social conditions.
3. Aged — Government policy — Canada.
I. Title.

HQ1064.C3B3 1987   305.2'6'0971   C87-094738-9

TABLE OF CONTENTS

CHAPTER 4: AGING AND SOCIAL POLICY 77

CHAPTER 5: THE FUTURE ELDERLY 111

ILLUSTRATIONS

TABLES

PREFACE

Social gerontology has developed into a growing field of academic study and policy concern. As the population ages in industrialized countries, and as academics and policy-makers themselves grow older, it becomes important to understand how the aging process is influenced by social, economic, and political variables and how population aging influences policy decisions. Governments are particularly concerned about the allocation of scarce resources to this growing segment of the population, especially one that uses a disproportionate share of social-security budgets.

In Canada our connotations of aging have been relatively negative. We have idolized youth and beauty and have developed many of our social institutions to suit the needs of young adults. Since the 1950s we have increasingly made older workers redundant and have raised old-age pension benefits. As a society, we are now in the expensive positon of watching the average age of retirement decline while the cost of pension benefits rises. Although the proportion of children in the population is shrinking, the proportion of elderly people is increasing. These demographic trends are leading to new controversies about future services, facilities, and benefits for the elderly.

The demographic and policy changes resulting from the aging population will have profound consequences for the structure of society. We may not only see an increase in nursing homes and chronic-care hospitals but also major changes in the delivery of health care for the elderly. Pension reform, which is already beginning, will affect young and old, those working for pay and those doing housework. The structure of work will have to change to accommodate an aging labour force and top-heavy organizations, as well as the two-income family. No longer can advertising and business gear their products and services to the teenage market, ignoring older consumers. Rising life expectancies and a larger proportion of elderly people in the population will transform our prejudices about old age and make us more aware of the needs and capabilities of older people.

As an introduction to social gerontology, this text presents a survey of social psychological, demographic, and policy-oriented research to the Canadian student. Although the book covers a wide variety of theoretical perspectives, the focus is on *macro-sociology* and the policy implications of these socio-economic changes.

In preparing this text, I would like to extend my appreciation to Colette Duquette and Kathleen Ippersiel for typing the manuscript. The anonymous reviewers, as well as Lorne Tepperman and David Tippin, provided invaluable constructive criticisms. I am grateful for their assistance. My colleagues at the Research Branch of the Library of Parliament offered encouragement for this project, but the ideas in this book are my own and should not be associated with the Research Branch.

Maureen Baker, Ph.D. (Sociology)
Research Branch
Library of Parliament
Ottawa
October 1987

1

THE MEANING OF AGING

INTRODUCTION

It has often been said that North America is a youth-oriented society. Certainly while the "baby-boomers" were growing up in the 1950s and 1960s, money was poured into building schools and other facilities for children and adolescents. Advertising focused on the under twenty-five market. To increase one's chances of success one had to be young, or at least present a youthful appearance, and "never trust anyone over thirty" became a popular slogan. The youth culture was especially demanding on women. They were encouraged to "lift" their faces and "tuck" their tummies, but balding men were not exempt from the pressure to recreate a youthful image with hair transplants. Now, however, the postwar baby-boom generation is approaching forty and middle age.

Concerns about youthful appearance are now juxtaposed with discussions about Registered Retirement Savings Plans. As the average age of Canadians and Americans rises, some of the emphasis on youthfulness and facilities for the young is giving way to a more realistic portrayal of the aging process, a new respectability for middle age, and debates on pensions and mandatory retirement. Although some of Canada's major institutions such as schools and hospitals were established to service a youthful population, they must now reorganize and accommodate an aging population.

Since the mid-1960s North American and European birth rates have fallen. Life expectancies have increased with improvements in nutrition, sanitation, and health care. The average age in many Western industrialized countries is rising, leading to a larger middle-aged and older population. With these demographic trends, politicians and bureaucrats, in the face of persistent public pressure, are revising social and economic programs for the elderly. Competing demands now exist for public money that was previously spent on elementary schools, family allowances, and youth-oriented programs. Furthermore, these demographic changes are forcing us to rethink our stereotypes of the aging process and the character

1

of older persons. The assumed passivity of elderly people is especially being challenged.

As an introduction to the sociology of aging, this book focuses on social policy concerns yet attempts to provide the student with a cross-section of issues in the field of social gerontology. We believe that the most important variables explaining the conditions of elderly people are not physiological or based on chronological age, but rather are aspects of the socio-economic structures of society that deprive people of power and control over their lives. Although the research, demographic data, and policy issues outlined in the following chapters orient this book to the Canadian student audience, cross-cultural material is also presented. Students who wish to delve more deeply into specific issues can refer to the many articles and books listed in the Bibliography.

Since aging affects all of us, it is not surprising that there has been growing interest in social gerontology courses at the college and university level. This text provides a general introduction to research and policy issues about aging, focusing on social policy concerns. In Chapter 1 we draw on social psychological studies to discuss the meaning of aging on a personal level and to indicate that the experience of aging varies by gender, social class, and cultural differences. A thorough understanding of the aging experience is essential for policy-makers planning for an aging society. Chapter 2 analyses demographic changes in Canadian society compared to other nations and the implications of population aging to societal institutions and opportunities. In Chapter 3 we look at historical trends in the status of the elderly with industrialization and modernization. The changing status of the elderly in Canada is outlined, comparing patterns of education, work, income, health, and lifestyles with those of other age groups. Chapter 4 provides an overview of historical trends in retirement policies, pensions, and the Canadian health-care system, comparing government attempts to improve the status of the elderly in Canada and in other countries. In the last chapter we review changing life transitions and social trends and compare the present elderly to the baby-boom generation in its future old age. The future elderly, we predict, will differ in many respects from today's elderly because of changing social trends in child rearing, divorce, labour force participation, and social-security benefits. In bringing together social psychological, demographic, economic, and policy concerns in one text, we have tried to indicate that the study of aging must be multidisciplinary and requires an understanding of historical trends as well as cross-cultural variations.

In Chapter 1 we will begin by defining the aspects of aging studied within the field of gerontology. We will then outline some of the sociological theories of aging. But most of the chapter will focus on the different experiences of aging in terms of personality changes, health needs, life satisfaction, and relationships from the point of view of men and women from varying socio-economic levels and different cultural groups. Although aging is a physiological process, it is influenced and even accelerated by certain attitudes and behaviours and the interaction between them. As our society ages, policy decisions will have to accommodate more older people, but in order to make fair and effective decisions, we need to understand the aging experience from a variety of social and cultural perspectives.

ASPECTS OF AGING

In the study of aging or *gerontology,* we can discuss chronological, biological, psychological, and social aging. Our legal rights and obligations are affected by chronological age or how many years we have lived. We have to be a certain age before we can enrol in school and we cannot leave school until a certain age. Chronological age influences whether or not we are punished for certain criminal acts and when we can apply for a driver's licence, drink alcohol, be drafted into the army, marry without our parents' consent, retire from work, or draw an old-age pension. Chronological age is used as a rough indicator of emotional maturity, physical development, or social need. But because it is based on general criteria, it cannot account for individual differences in maturity or capacity. The mature and politically aware fifteen-year-old is still not allowed to vote in Canada. The age at which a person is considered responsible or eligible for certain rights, however, varies by country, province, situation, and historical era.

Biological aging refers to physiological changes such as greying hair, balding, differences in metabolism, wrinkling skin, and declining strength and dexterity. Biological aging is of interest to sociologists and psychologists primarily because it affects our self-perception, our self-esteem, and how others treat us. If we are elderly, the community may protect us, pass over us when looking for expertise, or segregate us from the community in an old-age institution. In this book we will not examine the physiological aspects of aging in any detail, instead we will focus on psychological and social aging.

Psychological aging refers to cognitive, intellectual, and emotional development with increasing chronological age. It also involves the analysis of stability or change in personality, interests, attitudes, and lifestyle over time. As people mature, marry, raise children, grow older, and retire, their outlook on life often changes. They may become less flexible in their attitude to social or political trends and more established in their personal habits. As they age, they may adopt a more sedentary and family-oriented lifestyle. Differences in the attitudes and outlook of older people compared to younger people and the inner experience of growing old form part of the study of psychological aging.

How people age and how they feel about the process of aging varies with their gender, their health, their lifestyle, and the attitudes of those around them. People from wealthier backgrounds often appear and act younger than poorer people of the same chronological age. Certainly this is influenced by differences in diet, exercise, quality of clothing, and living conditions. But how one feels at a certain chronological age also depends on activities considered appropriate, self-esteem, and personal values. However, psychological variables such as self-esteem are very closely tied to sociological variables like social class. By this we are suggesting that living in a certain type of residential area, earning a particular income, and mixing with people from similar socio-economic circumstances are likely to influence the way others treat us and consequently the way we feel about ourselves.

Social aging refers to how people of different ages are treated by others or how various societies deal with the elderly. The status of the elderly compared to younger people can be analysed, and status differences among the elderly based on gender, ethnicity, race, or social class can be investigated. Social aging also involves a discussion of *socialization,* or the complex learning process by which individuals learn how to behave and participate in social life. Although most direct socialization takes place during childhood, both at home and in school, socialization is actually a lifelong process. At all ages, people develop and re-adjust their attitudes, motivations, and behaviour to their life experiences and material circumstances.

Cultural norms tell us how we should behave at a certain age, and how we should behave with others older or younger than ourselves. These norms differ from one society to another, from one historical period to another, and within cultural groups, but are important to learn while growing up. For example, parents often socialize their children and control their behaviour by saying "big boys don't cry," "young ladies don't run," or "act your age." Even though we are physically ready to engage in a behaviour, our parents or friends may tell us we are not *old enough* or are *too old.* For example, our parents may tell us that we are not old enough to marry at nineteen. But in some cultures if a women is not married by that age, she would be considered an "old maid." Another example of a cultural norm is the idea that it is inappropriate for a woman to marry a man considerably younger, but it is acceptable for a man to marry a younger woman. These norms, however, are constantly challenged and modified, even within generations.

Cultural norms also guide our treatment of others who are older or younger than ourselves. While we might call people of our own age group by their given names when we first meet, we hesitate to do so with older people. Titles of respect such as Mr., Mrs., or Dr. are considered more appropriate. Even when we are tired, we still feel obligated to give our seat on the bus to a senior citizen out of courtesy or respect for older people. The idea of respecting one's elders, however, appears to have eroded over recent years as younger people gain more education than their parents and as formalities are considered old-fashioned in many aspects of life. Yet within certain ethnic groups, such as Chinese and Native communities, respect for elders remains a significant part of cultural norms, which have persisited despite the low economic status of the elderly.

For both sexes in North America, growing old has generally been seen in a negative light in comparison to youth (Palmore, 1982). This is especially true for women, who are taught and encouraged by each other to lie about their ages and to disguise their physical aging process with hair dyes, foundation garments, and skin creams. Both sexes have been forced to retire from work, usually at age sixty-five, on the assumption either that they cannot function reliably after sixty-five or that it is more important to create vacancies for young people than to continue working. Since social status is generally linked to work in North America, retirement has often meant a drop in social status as well as income. This loss in income and status with old age often reduces self-esteem.

Increasingly, our society segregates people from each other on the basis of age. Prior to compulsory education in the late nineteenth century, children worked at home with their parents or other adults, or studied in a one-room school with a small number of children of all ages. Many parents worked at home, on the farm, or in the family business. Older people generally worked until they became disabled, and then were cared for by their spouse, by younger family members, or by a charitable organization. Now, children spend much of their day in large schools graded by age. Many parents go to a factory or office and do not see their children from morning until evening. Older workers retire from their jobs and spend more time in leisure pursuits on their own or with their friends. Some elderly people even live in specialized apartments or nursing homes and mix infrequently with younger people. In modern day urban society, age segregation is pronounced, but a considerable amount of social interaction still exists among the generations. Increasing segregation, however, does create some social distance and the potential for increased conflict between generations.

Both social and psychological aging form the bases of research and theory in social gerontology. Social scientists are interested in comparing the status of elderly and younger age groups, as well as investigating the attitudes and interactions of older people. Social gerontology is a relatively recent field that has drawn on various theoretical perspectives within the social sciences for its theories. For this reason, there are many theories of aging — each emphasizing a different aspect of the lifelong process.

Aging, as physical maturity and social psychological development, is certainly a lifelong process. In this book, however, we will focus on *old age* as it is generally defined in social science literature and for the purposes of government pension benefits.

GERONTOLOGY AS A FIELD OF STUDY

Some Theories of Aging

Although early research and practice in gerontology tended to focus on the individual and to be problem-oriented, the field has expanded rapidly in recent years and has become more theoretically diverse. While earlier studies had a strong social psychology orientation and were concerned with the problems people face as they age in industrial societies (Neysmith and Edwardh, 1984), present research is also being done on a societal level within the context of structural sociology and economics. Recently, systematic investigations have analysed relations between the social conditions of the elderly and the economy, the state, and the family. For example, the effects of the modernization process on the social status of the elderly and the historical and economic factors influencing social policy are important topics in the field of aging today. This has been called the *political economy of aging,* and it will receive more attention in this book than other approaches to the topic.

As with any social behaviour, there can be no single all-encompassing theory of aging, but rather different theories emphasizing aspects of the aging experience or the status of the elderly. Although social scientists searched for such a theory in the earlier stages of the discipline, they are now more likely to realize that the elderly are not a homogeneous group, but vary considerably by gender, class, ethnicity, geographic location, age, and state of health. Growing old has similar physiological characteristics throughout the world, but it is a different experience depending on many social, political, and economic conditions. Yet studies still dwell on industrialized societies, suggesting erroneously that aging is not an issue in developing countries (Neysmith and Edwardh, 1984).

Some theorists, focusing on social interaction and psychological variables, have investigated long-term personality changes, role transition, and interpersonal resources with increasing age. For example, activity theory suggests that as people lose a social role, such as worker or parent, they need to replace it with a new one in order to "successfully" age (Havighurst, 1968; Novak, 1985). The retired man, for instance, may need to find new hobbies and keep busy as a substitution for his lost role as worker. A recent widow may need to develop new friendships or focus more attention on her children or grandchildren to replace her lost husband. But the research on the relationship between activity level and life satisfaction is contradictory and complicated by gender and class differences. Having intimate relationships seems to be more important than the number of relationships or activities (Roadburg, 1985), and the type of activity in old age is closely related to former occupational and class-based activities.

Disengagement theory (Cumming et al., 1960; Cumming and Henry, 1961) argues that, contrary to activity theory, it is normal for aging people to gradually drop out of active participation in society. Critics, however, have shown that this disengagement process, which is supposed to be universal, actually depends on previous activity level and social class and is often forced on elderly people through retirement policies and lack of social services. Disengagement is also found to be possible in one aspect of life, such as work, while the person remains active in other aspects (Streib and Schneider, 1972).

The continuity theory postulates that personality tends to persist as a person grows older, despite life events (Neugarten et al., 1968). Many older people, however, are able to maintain a relatively stable environment, which largely explains personality stability. Those who are affected by divorce, death of a spouse, or some other major event sometimes experience substantial changes in lifestyle and personality. Changes in lifestyle are especially necessitated by a drop in income or death of a spouse.

The life-span approach looks at the role of the social environment in producing a healthy sense of identity and social competence. Phenomenological theories of aging emphasize the meaning attributed to growing old by the elderly and have emerged from social interactionism (Gubrium, 1973; Marshall, 1975; Decker, 1980). Adjustment theory examines people's reaction to retirement, suggesting that it depends on one's hierarchy of goals, especially the importance of work compared to other aspects of life (Atchley, 1976b). Men's adjustment to retirement has been viewed as more difficult than women's because of the primacy of work in men's lives.

These micro-level theories, which emphasize social interaction and personality, have only been partially successful in explaining aspects of the aging process because they do not seriously consider variables external to the individual such as cultural norms, environmental changes, social policy, and economic trends. By emphasizing individual attitudes and personality traits, they have not tried to compare the elderly with other age groups or look at historical changes in the aging process or status of the elderly. This task has been left to other theorists and researchers. However, many of the interactionist theories have been successful in portraying that the elderly are not passive recipients of the behaviour of others, but rather negotiate their status.

Macro-level theories of aging, which use entire societies or segments of society as units of analysis, have generally compared the elderly to other age categories in society. The aged have been discussed as a minority group in an attempt to compare the elderly to other disadvantaged groups and to explain their reaction to their social status. But this approach has been criticized for assuming that the elderly form a distinct group with characteristics that set them apart from younger age groups (Abu-Laban and Abu-Laban, 1977). The elderly have also been labelled a "subculture" with similar beliefs, attitudes, or behavioural styles (Rose, 1965). But differences exist among ethnic groups and social classes, and uniformity among the elderly may be more apparent than real.

Exchange theory of aging suggests that as people age, they lose their bargaining power compared to younger age groups. Technological changes and increased levels of education for younger generations have encouraged policies such as mandatory retirement, based on a preference for younger workers. Without paid work older people's incomes fall, and in a society where status is based largely on income, the elderly are less likely to be considered socially significant (Dowd, 1975). Those with money, property, social position, or specialized skills or knowledge can maintain their respect, prestige, and bargaining power. Many elderly people, however, have nothing to bargain with for respect except their former accomplishments or a claim to reciprocity from their offspring (Martin, 1971).

Conflict theory of aging suggests that generational differences exist that encourage conflict between age groups (Tindale and Marshall, 1980; Binstock, 1983). For example, unemployed young people often oppose the concept of job security or tenure. Similarly, while middle-aged people want more promotional opportunities to be opened up through early retirement policies, older people who want to keep their jobs may be lobbying for the abolition of mandatory retirement. According to conflict theory, increased youth unemployment and an aging population will lead to increased generational conflict. There is little empirical evidence either in Canada or the United States, however, that conflict between generations is more prevalent than within generations. Class conflict, ethnic differences, or regional differences are often more pronounced. But conflict certainly exists between organizations catering to youth and those focusing on the elderly population as they compete for scarce public resources and fight hard for their own priorities.

Modernization theories have suggested that the status of the elderly varies with the level of societal modernization, either inversely or with a curvilinear relationship (Cowgill and Holmes, 1972; Palmore and Manton, 1974). Industrialization necessitates the development of new technical skills gained largely by young people. The social treatment of the elderly worsens as their skills become obsolete and their educational levels decline relative to youth. But in post-industrial society, the experience and managerial skills of older workers become more economically useful and the status of the elderly rises. Increased longevity and lower birth rates typical of advanced industrialized societies also grant more power to older people as they become more numerous in the popula. Chapter 3 we will look more closely at this type of theory.

Environmental theories of aging have illustrated the ways in which one's cultural and physical environment affects attitudes, life satisfaction, or the physical aging process (Bruhn, 1971). Living in a particular neigh- bourhood or building alters friendships and visiting patterns, for example, which could influence life satisfaction. Severe winter weather can also restrict the mobility of older people and keep them house-bound or can become the main reason for the annual migration of elderly Canadians to Florida or more permanent migration to the West Coast in search of milder weather. These are all examples of issues dealt with by environ- mental theories of aging.

Demographers have looked for patterns in morbidity and mortality between cohorts, or people born at the same time. Probabilities of illness or death have been calculated throughout the entire life span of different cohorts. A central debate in gerontology is called the *rectangularization thesis,* which suggests that if we drew a graph of the probabilities of illness and death from birth to death, it would be rectangular in shape for both morbidity and mortality. How these curves will change in the future, however, is the subject of considerable controversy. Part of the debate relates to the maximum potential life span, which some argue is expandable and others say is fixed (Simmons-Tropea and Osborn, 1987). We will discuss this and further demographic controversies in the next chapter.

As in other fields, the search for an all-encompassing theory has proven to be futile in gerontology. Rather than trying to explain the aging process in general, most recent theories or empirical studies have focused on a specific aspect of aging. One aspect, for example, involves demographic projections based on morbidity and mortality and their implications for health care. Another involves sorting out the effects of aging from his- torical and environmental influences in passing through the life cycle. Another aspect relates to understanding the social and economic con- ditions that influence the status of the elderly relative to other groups. Social scientists have also analysed how societies deal with the aging process and elderly people. Each theory of aging looks at the process from a slightly different perspective, depending on the priorities and assumptions of the social scientist who initiated it. These assumptions relate to the nature of social reality, human motivation, and the impor- tance of social structure. While some theories use the individual as the unit of analysis, others use entire societies or age categories. Aging the- ories, therefore, can be grouped according to theoretical perspectives within the social sciences in general.

Although we mention many theories of aging in this book, we give more emphasis and credence to the "macro" theories because they take

.tion the economic, political, and social influences
uals. In particular, we favour the political economy
:ause they are historical and cross-cultural, and we
explain the negotiation involved in the development
we will illustrate in Chapter 4.

:search in Gerontology

Chrono.._ .ge is a very important variable in most social science
research. Political opinion polls, for example, generally compare people
of different ages to see if younger or older people feel differently about
particular social or political issues. How people cope with divorce might
involve comparisons between age groups as well as by gender, ethnicity,
and social class. Whether or not senior citizens will require more chronic-
care facilities in the future may be influenced not only by their health
status but also by the proportions of older elderly people in the population. However, we cannot really conclude anything about the effects
of the aging process from these studies, or even what causes attitude or
behavioural variations by age. We can only say that people at different
chronological ages and from varying ethnic groups or social classes have
different opinions, behaviours, or social service needs. This can be very
useful information for political parties or social service agencies, but less
illuminating from the point of view of the theoretical social scientist.

Although one very effective way to study aging would be to follow a
group of people through their entire life span, this kind of longitudinal
study is very costly and time-consuming. Furthermore, it does not lead
to very immediate results in the form of reports or publications. For this
reason, empirical researchers often use a cross-sectional design that involves
comparing different age groups on one or more occasions. It is difficult
to know from this type of research design, however, whether aging causes
people to think or behave differently or if they are different because of
other events or factors. The same problem is inherent with cohort analysis, in which the behaviour or attitudes of people born in certain years
or who married at the same time are compared.

As with many social science studies, much of the research in gerontology has been based on white middle-class subjects who are more
readily available to university-based researchers. In past studies of retirement, for example, males were most often used as "subjects" and retirement was assumed to be a different experience for men and women even
before any research was done. Women's adjustment to their spouse's
retirement has even been equated with their own retirement (Thurnher,
1974), and assumptions have been made that work and therefore retirement are less salient for women (Barnett and Baruch, 1978–79). Gen-
eralizing from unrepresentative samples is a serious methodological error
because it gives us a false impression about the nature of social reality.

If broader or comparative samples were used, results could differ substantially.

The need for rapport in studies using interviewing is particularly important but could be difficult in gerontology. Keeping older people on topic, relying on their memory, and dealing with hearing problems prove to be specific difficulties. Yet any category of people provides some challenges for researchers. Young children, for example, are also difficult to study because of their shorter attention span, their inability to read, and the necessity to obtain permission from parents to involve them in a research project. Despite elderly people's lack of familiarity with methods and standard types of questions, participation rates in survey research tend to be relatively high for elderly people compared to other age groups. Most people enjoy talking about themselves, especially those who are not particularly busy with work.

Although more popular among historians, oral histories have been used by social scientists to study the elderly. One example is Peter Li's study of Chinese immigrants in Saskatchewan (Li, 1985). Relying on older people's memories and developing a valid framework for organizing the case histories are two problems with this research method. Yet if we accept the theoretical idea that reality is socially constructed or that if people believe events to be real, they are real in their social consequences, oral histories can provide a valid measure of aspirations, anxieties, and attitudes, as well as changing social conditions.

Using historical research methods rather than interviews or questionnaires avoids many of the problems of rapport or memory. Historical documents can reveal how the elderly lived in former eras. Statistics can provide basic information about mortality rates, participation in the labour force, and retirement ages, but little information about interpersonal relations or how people felt about the aging process. As with any topic in social science, the type of research method and the initial assumptions about what is important to study will influence the findings.

Gerontology is a rapidly developing academic field in North America. In Canada, however, there are fewer nation-wide or longitudinal projects than in the United States because of the smaller size of the research community and the nature of past funding practices, and because gerontology is still a nascent field of study. Canada still has no centralized agency to support gerontological research in health and social sciences, but research centres and gerontology programs and associations have developed across the country. The Canadian Association of Gerontology, for example, was founded in 1971 and the *Canadian Journal on Aging* began in 1982. Both Health and Welfare Canada and the Social Sciences and Humanities Research Council have targeted research funds to gerontology (Marshall, 1987:5, 6). Until recently, social gerontology texts relied heavily on American research that tended to focus on a social psychological approach. But now more Canadian research is available

Historical research can reveal how the elderly lived in former eras. (Public Archives Canada/PA 42915)

that combines the "micro" approach with a political economy perspective more typical of British or European gerontology.

In the remainder of this chapter we will examine the research findings on the aging experience, including personality changes, aging and health, sex differences in the significance of aging, changing patterns of life satisfaction, relationships among the elderly, and the process of bereavement. Most of these studies have a social psychological orientation; yet the implications are considerable for policy-makers. Social workers and health practitioners need more information on the process of aging and the lifestyles and attitudes of the elderly, and policy-analysts and politicians are increasingly interested in the implications of the aging population for social planning and political decision making. For this reason, the field is growing quickly and draws on a variety of academic disciplines. In order to make effective public policy in the field of aging, the student needs to be open to multidisciplinary analysis.

THE AGING EXPERIENCE

Personality Changes Over Time

One of the controversies in the research on aging deals with the extent of personality change experienced by people as they age. Researchers have noticed major differences in attitudes and outlook between age groups and have wondered if people develop their social and political attitudes as they mature or if different age cohorts have their personality patterns set for life by similar social and political experiences in the past.

Studies have found that the current cohort of older people typically is more conservative, cautious, egocentric, introverted, passive, and less emotional than younger age groups (McPherson, 1983:210). Much of the research suggests that this is not the inevitable result of aging but is caused by life events (Nicholson, 1980) or at least an interaction between personality and the social situation (Epstein, 1979). Changes in people's situation often cause attitudes to be modified. For example, the death of a spouse for whom one prayed for recovery could diminish religious feelings. The divorce of a child may liberalize parents' attitudes towards divorce or living together. A weak financial position upon retirement may heighten hostility to younger people earning high incomes. Retirement and bereavement are two events that especially lead to lifestyle and attitudinal changes because they require major modifications of habits. But many lesser situational factors can influence personality, attitudes, and world view. There is some agreement in the research, however, that most people do not undergo major personality transformations as they age even though many experience minor changes (Thomae, 1976; McCrae and Costa, 1984).

Social gerontology has tried to sort out the physiological and psychological aspects of aging from cohort differences. For example, do people automatically become less physically active as they approach old age, or were older people brought up with different attitudes about sports and the importance of exercise? Part of the lack of clarity in the research arises from the methodology chosen for studies. It is easier and less expensive to study different age groups at one point in time and ask about earlier influences in their lives than to follow changes in the same individuals over their lifetime. But in addition to this, many past studies focused on white middle-class institutionalized Americans who were more accessible subjects of research to the neglect of other groups. When we discuss the status of the elderly in Chapter 3, we will highlight ethnic variations in the behaviour and status of elderly people.

Generations raised in the same era, who experience similar social and political events, develop attitudes that generally last for a lifetime. For example, those who were raised in Canada during the 1930s Depression often share conservative attitudes about financial security. On the other hand, later generations raised during the boom of the 1960s, with social experimentation, full employment, and well-developed social-security programs are often less concerned with financial security and more liberal in their social attitudes. Attitudinal differences between age groups, however, must certainly be explained both by the experience gathered in moving through the life cycle — marriage, childbearing, child rearing, retirement, and bereavement — and by being raised during particular historic events and with certain prevalent values.

Several studies have found that gender roles become less distinct with age (Abu-Laban, 1978; Troll and Parron, 1981). Older men often become more interested in family and relationships, less concerned with sports and physical prowess, and more willing to perform domestic work after retirement. Similarly, women often become more independent and assertive, less conforming in terms of fashion and appearance, and less concerned about pleasing others as they age. In the case of retired men, more leisure time gives them the opportunity to play with their grandchildren, cook, shop, or visit with friends. Diminishing physical strength undermines confidence in their own abilities and makes them less willing to appear in control. On the other hand, women are frequently widowed by age sixty-five and sometimes are forced to develop new skills out of necessity such as caring for a car and doing minor repairs on the house. Developing new skills often increases women's self-esteem and confidence while retirement from paid work and diminishing physical strength places men and women on a more equal footing.

Neither the aging process alone nor the social and political experiences of particular cohorts can adequately explain why older people often display different attitudes and behaviour than younger persons. Rather, both of these factors are influential. Furthermore, we now know that not all categories of people are influenced in the same way by life events. More cross-cultural and longitudinal studies with representative or random samples need to be done to accurately answer questions of personality and aging as well as other issues, such as whether physical activity need decline so much with increasing age. Several recent Canadian studies meet the above criteria such as the longitudinal study at the Centre on Aging at the University of Manitoba, the work on ethnicity and aging by Ujimoto (1987) and Driedger and Chappell (1987), and the Ontario Longitudinal Study of Aging by the Ontario Department of Public Welfare.

Aging and Health

In this section we will mention some of the research related to how elderly people feel about their health, but we will not discuss the health-care system itself or demographic studies predicting future morbidity. Instead, demographic predictions will be analysed in Chapter 2 on the *Aging Canadian Population*, and the health status of older people will be compared to younger people in Chapter 3 on the *Changing Status of the Elderly*. Policy issues concerning health will be discussed in Chapter 4 on *Aging and Social Policy*. In this chapter we are focusing only on social psychological issues such as studies of health expectation, mental health, and the relationship between life satisfaction and health.

The physical effects of aging is a topic more appropriately studied within medical science and physiology than the social sciences, but phys- ical aging is closely related to attitudes and social practices. The lack of regular, vigorous exercise, for example, hastens the physiological aging process (Wiswell, 1980; Smith and Serfass, 1981; Shephard, 1984). Con- tinued exercise from an early age increases longevity and the likelihood of good health, aids recovery from some diseases, and prolongs psycho- logical and physical independence for the elderly. Numerous studies have reported a decline in physical activity after people leave high school, which is especially noticeable for women, working-class people, and those in rural areas (Statistics Canada, 1978:10; Hall and Richardson, 1983:53). This inactivity with increasing age may be caused by the lack of sports facilities, potential teammates, or time; or attitudes that designate sports and physical activity as childish or unimportant (McPherson, 1983:176). Whatever the cause, lack of exercise certainly accelerates the deterioration of physical health.

Despite no clear objective evidence that men are healthier than women, elderly women report more health problems (Chappell et al., 1986). This may be another indication of women's greater willingness to admit weak- ness, problems, or illness and to be more attuned to symptoms before they become serious. Older men, on the other hand, are more likely to say they feel fine until they need to be hospitalized or die suddenly. "Macho" behaviour is definitely unrewarding if we compare mortality rates of men and women of similar ages throughout the life span.

Perception of good health is clearly one of the factors that encourages older people to report high levels of life satisfaction. But some researchers have argued that the elderly generally have low expectations of health because of the negative stereotypes of the aging process and elderly peo- ple. Older people compare themselves to these stereotypes and feel rel- atively well off. They therefore rate their own health as good, even when they experience chronic health problems (Chappell, 1987).

Poorer people experience more health problems than richer people throughout life (Wilkins and Adams, 1983; Hirdes, Brown, and Forbes, 1986; Regush, 1987). Poor nutrition, lack of knowledge about health care, inferior housing and working conditions, and lack of access to medical facilities lead to a variety of physical and mental health problems. Particularly as they age, the poor, the non-white, and those with lower education are more susceptible to poor health than those with more financial and educational resources. For older people who can afford to pay for food, however, shopping may be a problem, and denture or digestive difficulties may cause them to avoid certain foods. Lack of interest in eating may also be caused by depression and loneliness, which are experienced by all socio-economic levels.

Few longitudinal studies have been done in this country on health, and mental health is particularly under-researched. Many of the psycho- logical disorders thought to be prevalent among the elderly such as

depression

depression are actually more common in adolescence or middle age. Unlike physical health, there is no clear age trend for mental illness (D'Arcy, 1987). Although much attention has been paid to mental health problems and high rates of suicide among youth, suicide rates for males peak at ages twenty to twenty-four and again at forty-five to sixty-four. For females, rates increase with age and peak at forty-five to sixty-four, but at all ages male rates are higher than female rates (Lapierre, 1984:54; D'Arcy, 1987). To many people, suicide among older people appears less upsetting than among youth who have yet to live their lives. But high rates among the middle-aged and elderly are indicative of depression, diminishing life interest, and fear of becoming helpless. The lower rates of suicide among older women may indicate more realistic life goals, greater ability to express emotions, closer ties with family and friends, or more acceptance of dependence in aging. While feminists have argued that these characteristics do not lead to high socio-economic status, they seem to help women live longer.

Some elderly people, especially the poor, less educated, and immigrants, hesitate to seek medical advice for health problems because they fear or dislike doctors, or feel that doctors do not have time for them. Few doctors have been trained to care for the elderly and some are noticeably less interested in older patients. The Canadian health-care system, which is heavily physician-oriented, actually discourages doctors from spending time with patients of any age (Chappell et al., 1986). Since doctors bill through Medicare on a fee for service basis, they earn less money if they prolong a visit by discussing lifestyle, diet, or even the details of a medical procedure. Other health-care practitioners, who work for a salary and therefore have time to discuss health issues with their patients, are less often consulted because they are not always covered by government health insurance. Since doctors seldom make house calls any more, elderly people are forced to wait in the doctor's office for a visit that might last only a few minutes. In Chapter 4 we will discuss the Canadian health system in detail, some policy implications of the present system, and suggestions for reform.

Sex Differences in the Significance of Aging

Our attitudes about the significance and consequences of physiological aging differ for males and females. Since a high value is placed on women's youthful appearance, it is not surprising that they spend considerable time and money attempting to appear younger than their chronological age. Some feminists have argued that because women have been defined essentially in terms of their sexuality and fertility, growing old is more consequential to them (de Beauvoir, 1970; Dulude, 1978:4–5). Although some attitudes towards women's roles have changed, an older woman may still be taken more seriously in a managerial or professional role if she is also attractive, expressive, and maternal. In other words, feminists argue persuasively that the double-standard of aging persists.

In professional and managerial occupations, growing old is synonymous with gaining knowledge or wisdom, and appearing too youthful is perceived to be a disadvantage. In manual labour jobs or sports activities, on the other hand, diminished strength or speed spells the end of that phase of work. But the older male worker can sometimes move up to supervisor or manager, and the male athlete can become a coach or businessman. Fewer options have been available for women whose occupations rely on youth or fertility. Those women who are hired as receptionists, models, or who work as homemakers, for example, often perceive growing old as threatening to their very existence. As long as youth, beauty, and fertility continue to be held in high regard for women, physiological aging will generate a more serious personal crisis for women than for heterosexual men. For homosexual men without a partner, aging can precipitate a similar reaction as it sometimes does for women. Finding sexual partners is largely based on physical attractiveness in the male gay community, and aging gay men who have no permanent partner may be at a competitive disadvantage with younger men. This does not necessarily mean, however, that there are significant differences in the life satisfaction of gay and non-gay older men (Lee, 1987).

To be old and female has been called a "double jeopardy" (Chappell and Havens, 1980; Posner, 1980) because the disadvantages of being a female multiply with increasing age. For example, low wages, lack of job security, and reduced fringe benefits eventually translate into fewer savings or a lower pension than retired men earn. Older women are not only more likely to be living below the poverty line than older men, but they are also far more likely to be widowed and living alone (National Council of Welfare, 1984b). The assumed loss of speed, dexterity, and strength with increasing age adds to existing prejudices about women's abilities. But this objective lower status does not appear to influence life satisfaction.

Havens and Chappell (1983) have confirmed that older ethnic women suffer objectively from a "triple jeopardy" because of their age, sex, and ethnicity. Yet they are no more likely than others to feel disadvantaged or to express lower satisfaction with their lives. Perhaps this is because they compare their own situation to other older ethnic women rather than to younger people in the larger society. From these studies, it is apparent that women do not always translate their objectively lower status to a psychological or subjective level, perhaps because they have grown used to inequality (Dulude, 1978:71). This has confused researchers in the past and has led to inconsistent findings in research on life satisfaction.

Early research on women and retirement focused on their adjustment to their husbands' retirement because paid work was considered to be less significant for women (Kline, 1975; Fengler, 1975; Barnett and Baruch, 1978–79). Contradictory findings are prevalent in the research concerning women's adjustment to their own retirement compared to men's adaptation (Atchley, 1976 a and b; Palmore et al., 1979; Skogland, 1979). While men's retirement has been described as difficult or traumatic, some researchers have argued that retirement is less consequential for women. Women's closer ties with friends and family and their continued responsibility for children and household tasks throughout their work lives have provided them with a continuity that extends beyond retirement.

Of the four hundred elderly people Gold interviewed in the Montreal area, the experience of aging appeared to be more difficult for women. Women in her study had lower levels of education and income, fewer were married, and more were widowed than their male counterparts. Gold found that these elderly women had lower levels of confidence in their abilities, more anxieties, and a greater perception that elderly people are badly off (Gold, 1984:34). These conclusions, however, are not entirely consistent with those cited above, which found that older women are objectively worse off but do not express dissatisfaction as often as men.

The retirement experience, therefore, depends on previous responsibilities, relationships, and interests as well as length of career, income, prestige, and marital status. The fact that most women workers have relatively low status and poorly paid jobs may make them more favourable towards retirement. Yet at the same time, their lower savings and pensions make retirement more difficult financially. We cannot assume that women are less committed to work than men, but there is evidence that women's closer ties with friends and family assist their emotional adjustment to old age and retirement, even though they are more likely than men to be widowed and poor (Connidis, 1982). As more women stay in the labour force for their entire working lives, researchers should be able to sort out more effectively potential gender differences in retirement experiences. But any research on this topic would have to consider work experience, status, and level of pay.

The factors that predict good psychological functioning for elderly women and men are essentially the same: higher levels of education, being married, good physical health, sufficient income, and social rewards for efforts and achievements. However, the two sexes do not necessarily define "sufficient" income in the same way and do not have equal access to resources. This leads to different experiences in the aging process for men and women.

Changing Patterns of Life Satisfaction

In studies of life satisfaction, a higher percentage of older people than younger people report that they are "very satisfied" with various aspects of their lives. From teenage years to age seventy, life satisfaction consistently increases (Atkinson, 1979; Cutler, 1979; Northcott, 1982). Even the low-income elderly report high levels of life satisfaction. There are several possible explanations for this trend. Firstly, aspirations are more often in line with one's current situation with advancing age. Major improvements in wealth and status are not expected by older persons, who tend to be relatively satisfied with what they have. Secondly, higher reported rates of life satisfaction among older people could be a cohort effect; historically, each generation could have lower expectations because of changing socio-economic circumstances such as high unemployment rates and inflation. Thirdly, retirement from work allows older people more leisure time to engage in their hobbies or meet with friends, which increases their life satisfaction. Fourthly, elderly people may report high levels of satisfaction because they do not want to complain or appear ungrateful or because they feel that circumstances are beyond their control (Roadburg, 1985:142). These feelings of fatalism could arise from earlier experiences such as the 1930s Depression and the Second World War, and would therefore be considered a cohort effect. Probably all of these factors contribute to the finding that reported life satisfaction increases with age.

Various theorists and practitioners have tried to find aspects of the social environment that affect the morale of elderly people. Gubrium (1973) argued that elderly people who are very active have higher morale when they live in an age-heterogeneous community. On the other hand, elderly people who are physically inactive have higher levels of morale when they live in segregated senior citizen communities. This implies that morale is affected by the abilities of those around us and how they mesh with our own abilities.

Based on a Manitoba sample of institutionalized elderly from 1971, Myles (1979) found that elderly people who live in age-homogeneous environments generally have higher morale, higher levels of social interation, and more satisfying relationships than those residing in the general community. In an environment planned for the elderly, there are more opportunities for social participation, equal social exchanges, and a supportive reference group; there is less emphasis on "productive" activities. Elderly people are consequently less likely to feel socially isolated when they are not constantly compared to younger people, their goals, and their lifestyles (Myles and Boyd, 1982). Other researchers have found, however, that living in their own homes rather than an institution leads to higher levels of reported satisfaction among the elderly (Chappell and Penning, 1979). This is partly because living at home gives the elderly more control over their daily schedules. But it is also true that those who choose to live at home tend to be healthier and need less assistance than those who live in a senior citizen home or institution (Smith and Lipman,

1972; Hulicka et al., 1975). Good health is another factor contributing to higher levels of life satisfaction as is access to transportation (Cutler, 1975; Carp, 1980).

Many studies have found that perceived good health is a primary factor influencing a positive life outlook among the elderly (Larson, 1978; Snider, 1980; Seleen, 1982; Roadburg, 1985; Lee, 1987). Poor health may curtail visiting and social relationships and may necessitate institutionalization. Living in an institution involves a certain amount of regimentation, and losing control over one's daily schedule is related to low levels of satisfaction among all age groups. One of the best predictors of life satisfaction, in fact, is self-rated health status, which involves subjective expectations of health, often compared to other people of similar age. Self-rated health is a better predictor of satisfaction than objective health status, socio-economic status, activity level, or social background (Snider, 1980; Chappell et al., 1986).

Life satisfaction may not necessarily coincide with external circumstances. Elderly rural dwellers often express greater satisfaction than elderly urban dwellers. Objectively, the rural elderly have lower socio-economic status, poorer health, fewer services, and poorer housing than urban people. But subjectively, their morale seems to be as high and they are as satisfied with their neighbourhoods (Lee and Lassey, 1980; Fengler and Jensen, 1981). Rural people, however, usually experience a lower cost of living, lower crime rates and perception of crime, and more interaction and assistance from neighbours (Fengler and Jensen, 1981).

Life satisfaction rises for both men and women after their children have left home. The "empty-nest syndrome," which in the past was assumed to be the cause of depression in middle-aged women, now appears to increase well-being among women (Palmore et al., 1979; Barnett and Baruch, 1978–79; George et al., 1980). The rate of labour force participation among women aged forty-five to sixty-four has increased considerably in the last decade and a qualitative shift appears to have taken place with regard to the meaning of work for women (Connidis, 1982). In the 1950s women in financial need composed a large portion of the female labour force, but now more middle-class women work for personal satisfaction and fulfillment as well as for financial reasons.

Working women compared to housewives generally report higher levels of life satisfaction and adjustment throughout the life cycle to old age (Lehr, 1978; George et al, 1980). Having their own money, enjoying daily contact with adults, and making some kind of contribution to society are reasons given for the higher satisfaction of working women. Housewives, on the other hand, express increased satisfaction when their retired husbands participate in household tasks (Hill and Dorfman, 1982). The lives of working husbands and homemaker wives tend to become increasingly separate with age. After the husband's retirement, his participation in domestic chores not only provides greater companionship for his wife but also equalizes the work-load. Otherwise, he would be idle and she would still be working.

For older men, life satisfaction has been related to higher social class and better health, rather than relationships with their children (Watson and Kivett, 1976:486). Because men usually do not develop close relationships throughout their lives, their children seldom enhance their life satisfaction after retirement. Retired men are consequently more likely than retired women to say that they miss "having something to do" (Roadburg, 1985:95). Older women, on the other hand, value relationships with their children, and these relationships have a more direct impact on their feelings of well-being. Retired women are more likely to miss the social contacts from their previous jobs, but both sexes place a high value on the social contact provided by the work environment after retirement (Harris et al., 1975; Parker, 1982; Roadburg, 1985). The fact that older men and women are deriving satisfaction from different areas of life may have confused the results of earlier studies that did not consider gender differences to be important to life satisfaction.

Several studies have indicated that contact with friends affects the life satisfaction of the elderly more than contact with relatives (Hess and Markson, 1980:280; Goudy and Goudreau, 1981:45). Other research, however, comes to the opposite conclusion (Brown, 1974; Reid and Ziegler, 1977; Thompson, 1978). These contradictory conclusions may simply be the result of differences in the gender of the subjects in the study, as women seem to have more meaningful contact with their kin. This indicates the overwhelming importance of including both men and women in any study of how life satisfaction changes throughout the aging process.

In a study of aging among gay men, Lee (1987) argues that there are few differences in life satisfaction between gay and heterosexual men. He suggests that the theory of accelerated gay aging is based largely on stereotypes and may reflect the lives of unattached gay men prior to the gay liberation movement. The same factors influence men's life satisfaction regardless of sexual preference: perception of health and adequate income, higher educational levels, and meaningful relationships.

Generally, the research on the elderly indicates that adjustment to aging depends on several situational variables: self-rated good health, the perception of adequate financial resources, and the perception of social support. But perceptions of adequate income and support vary by gender as well as by socio-economic backgound. Women appear to be satisfied with lower levels of income but place a high value on relationships with both friends and kin. Regardless of these variations in life satisfaction, elderly people still report higher levels of life satisfaction than younger age groups.

Life satisfaction is obviously a very subjective construct and is therefore difficult to study by looking at objective social or economic circumstances. Being satisfied with life relates to past experiences. We know that many of today's elderly suffered through a major depression, a world war, bouts of unemployment or illness, and ethnic or sexual discrimination. If they anticipated poverty in their old age and now receive an adequate pension, they may be satisfied, regardless of the actual level of their income. If they feared institutionalization in their old age and are still living at home receiving frequent visits from their children, they may be very satisfied. While younger people are healthier and have higher incomes, the elderly generally compare themselves to their peer group and consequently feel well-off (Larson, 1978; Neysmith, 1980).

Relationships and the Elderly

Despite popular ideas that the nuclear family is a relatively new institution, the three-generation household where elderly parents are supported by their children has always been an exception in North America (Laslett, 1971; Synge, 1980). The myth that families are now abandoning their elderly, a myth which has been perpetrated by the media, also needs to be emphatically refuted (Rosenthal, 1987), for elderly parents and their children still rely on each other for companionship and assistance, especially in times of crises. Moreover, many older people find it difficult to talk to strangers about personal matters or to hire professionals to perform personal care or household tasks, preferring to rely on family members. In fact, the elderly are more likely to turn to their family and friends for both emotional and concrete forms of support than to community services or professionals (Kaye, 1985; Chappell et al., 1986).

Family size, however, is declining and fewer children are available to help their aging parents now than a few generations ago. This trend has led to new pressures on families, and primarily on women, to care for their aging parents. Elderly women are especially dependent on their daughters for daily care. As issues related to aging become more prominent in the media, more cases of elderly abuse or "granny bashing" are reported even though the phenomenon is still relatively rare (Schlesinger, 1984). If home care is to be a viable alternative to institutionalization, considerable integration between family members and home-care workers needs to be negotiated, as family members sometimes feel professionals are interfering in their private domain and may subtlely sabbotage their efforts (Kaye, 1985). But more people are growing old without immediate family to care for them and may therefore require facility care in the future (Stolar et al., 1986). While family members express a willingness to care for older members, they are not always able to do so because of employment commitments or other family obligations (Rosenthal, 1987).

Married elderly people can often maintain their independence by taking care of each other. Perhaps for this reason, older married people generally report higher levels of life satisfaction than the widowed or single (Larson, 1978). Marital relationships also appear to become stronger in old age than in middle age. Several studies have found that there is a curvilinear relationship between length of marriage and marital satisfaction (Burr, 1970; Rollins and Feldman, 1970; Lupri and Frideres, 1981). Satisfaction peaks at the beginning of marriage, declines in the middle years, and rises again near the end of the relationship — after retirement. Abu-Laban (1978) indicated a number of similarities between the honeymoon period and the post-retirement phase. Both involve a child-free or adult-centered life, more discretionary time, a more egalitarian division of labour, and a heightened appreciation of the relationship because of its newness or the imminence of death.

Studies of marital satisfaction at different stages of marriage, however, are usually cross-sectional. Instead of studying couples for the duration of their marriage (a rather long-term, expensive, and unrewarding project in terms of publications), individuals married for varying lengths of time are compared. This may be an unfair comparison because older couples are "survivors" and those whose marriages did not last are not included in the study. Also, after being married for forty or more years, one might feel compelled to express satisfaction in the same way that recently married people are *expected* to be happy (Abu-Laban, 1978). It is difficult to assess whether expressed satisfaction with marriage is real or simply what the subjects think they should say.

In later life, relationships with siblings are weaker than relationships with children, even though people often renew contact with their siblings as they approach the end of their life (Scott, 1983). While female family linkages have often been strong throughout life, especially between sisters (Troll, 1971; Cicirelli, 1977), men who have spent little time with their siblings in the middle years tend to renew contact as they age. The never-married, divorced, and widowed generally have more contact with siblings than married people, since couples are often preoccupied with each other to the exclusion of friends and relatives. There has been little research, however, on the quantity, quality, or nature of sibling relationships during either the middle years or among the elderly (McPherson, 1983:335).

Contact with children and grandchildren varies by sex and social class. For example, working-class parents (particularly women) are more likely to live with their children, to exchange services (especially babysitting), and to visit with their children. Middle-class parents speak to their children on the telephone or write letters but are less likely than working-class parents to visit in person. Instead of exchanging services, middle-class elderly parents typically send money or gifts to their children and grandchildren (Shanas et al., 1967; Lopata, 1979; Neugarten, 1979; Synge et al., 1981). Mothers perceive their children as providing more emotional support than do fathers, and older women compared to older men more often use their children as confidants (Babchuk, 1978–79).

Now that more older women are in the labour force, they may have less time or interest in helping to raise their grandchildren. However among the working class, grandmothers are still involved in child rearing or babysitting. When both parents are working or when a parent has been divorced or separated, child care is essential but is often too costly to afford. Consequently family members, especially grandmothers, frequently provide this useful service. Various studies have found that the grandparent role is more salient for the working class; for widows; for less-educated people; for older, retired, or unemployed people; and for those less involved in community affairs (McPherson, 1983:345). By their very presence, grandparents may provide a sense of family continuity, acting as mediators of or deterrents to family disruption (Bengtson, 1985). Moreover, the grandparent role may become more important in the future with rising life expectancies, when more people will live to see their grandchildren become adults.

Although frequency of contact with children does not affect elderly women's feelings of well-being (Beaudoin et al., 1973; Arling, 1976; Weishaus, 1979), regular contact with friends and neighbours is important. But as people grow older, more of their friends and acquaintances die, and new friends are harder to make as life becomes more sedentary and income drops (Dulude, 1978). Senior citizen clubs, with government subsidies for space, transportation, and co-ordinators, help provide opportunities to develop new friendships and activities. Yet cross-sex friendships, which are more acceptable among the elderly than among young people, are still difficult because the sex ratio becomes imbalanced with age. Many senior citizen clubs are comprised largely of women who shower attention on the few male members. Considering the imbalance of the sex ratio, polygyny may be more appropriate for the elderly than monogamy!

Considerable research has been done on the relationship between informal social networks and well-being in later life, however, the nature of this relationship is still unclear. We know that children typically dominate the support networks of the elderly (Lopata, 1979; Shanas, 1979). Recent research has also distinguished between instrumental aid such as help with home repairs and expressive assistance provided by confidants to find out who is assisting elderly people (Cantor, 1979; Ward et al., 1982). However, the concept of "social support" has been inadequately conceptualized and operationalized in many studies, as it usually has been measured by the number of relationships rather than the fulfillment of needs (Lowenthal and Robinson, 1976; Thoits, 1982). Perception of need fulfillment should be the focus of these studies.

Even when friends and relatives are available to help, not all are equally supportive or can be relied upon in the same way. For example, if family members are available to assist the elderly, this may mean that the elderly do not make use of formal support such as housekeeping services, senior citizen homes, or visiting nurses, which are theoretically available to them. Evidence that social support contributes to well-being is neither strong nor consistent in the research, but perception of social support seems to be a better predictor of well-being. This relationship could be clarified by more careful attention to the various dimensions of the concept (Ward, 1985).

Bereavement and the Rituals of Death

Funerals are usually a time when families come together, forget their differences, and offer assistance to each other. Many people's religious beliefs include an afterlife or heaven, and reunions in the afterlife remain one of the themes of funerals. Flowers, subdued voices, dark colours, soft lights, and quiet music help form the setting for this final farewell. The social recognition of the finality of physical death is thereby reinforced.

Preoccupation with the imminence of death is a characteristic of some elderly people, which is often disturbing to younger family members. In our society, speaking openly about death makes people uncomfortable, so we construct euphemisms for death and dying, including "passing on," "resting," and "sleeping." Our rituals of death include adding make-up to a person's skin, arranging their hair, and dressing them in their best clothes for relatives and friends to see them in the coffin.

Formalized preparation for widowhood is as absent from our society as specific preparation for marriage or child rearing. We actually discourage people from talking about the potential death of their spouse and seldom encourage the development of future coping skills. Certain categories of people such as those whose spouse has undergone a prolonged illness may be better prepared to handle financial or other practical matters alone. But seldom do people anticipate the problems of widowhood before it actually happens, especially the loneliness on the anniversary of the death or other dates that used to mark family celebrations. Helena Lopata's research on widowhood (1973) highlighted the lack of preparation women have for living lives without their husbands (Reinharz, 1986).

Studies of bereavement have usually focused on women, since the ratio of widows to widowers in North America is 5 to 1 (Lopata, 1973, 1979; Harvey and Bahr, 1980; McPherson, 1983:348). For women who have centred their lives around husband and family, widowhood often involves a loss of identity and a perceived drop in status because women have typically gained status through marriage (Matthews, 1980). Widows are more likely than the married elderly to think of themselves as "old" and are also more inclined to be unhappy, to worry, and to anticipate death in the near future (Riley and Foner, 1968:353).

Researchers have investigated the various stages of bereavement, the patterns of adjustment, and the changing self-concept of the widow. The initial mourning period appears to be the most stressful and may last for over a year. Widows and widowers often experience contradictory emotions throughout this stage of bereavement, including disbelief, numbness, yearning, depression, anger, and guilt. The mourning stage may

Providing true palliative care difficult in Canada, MD says

By Caitlin Kelly
The Globe and Mail

There are 75 palliative care units in Canadian hospitals designed to provide care to dying patients, but resistance by provincial governments to establishing non-institutional facilities ensures the unique position of the Maison Michel Sarrazin, says Dr. Dorothy Ley, president of the Palliative Care Foundation.

The notion of a hospice, a free-standing building unattached to a hospital, began in the late fifties and early sixties in England with St. Christopher's House in London, which was established by Dr. Cicely Saunders to support dying patients and their families both physically and emotionally.

In moving across the Atlantic, the idea of hospice care has substantially changed from that of a separate centre to services within hospitals, nursing homes or the community, Dr. Ley says.

"The semantics have gotten out of hand," says Dr. Ley, whose 5-year-old national non-profit group works to promote humane and compassionate care for the dying.

A "very interesting and superb example of hospice care," the Maison Michel Sarrazin is unique, she says.

"This is the way one should do it."

But trying to provide true hospice care in Canada is difficult, despite a growing interest in the treatment of the terminally ill and the development of many excellent in-hospital programs, she says.

"The philosophy of health care in this country doesn't easily allow for the provision of care outside hospitals. It has never been done and there's great resistance at all levels of provincial government to this type of activity."

The problems include finding the money to build the hospices, obtaining operating funds and the inevitable drain on existing community services created by any hospice, Dr. Ley says.

"It's not possible to buy a house and put sick people into it without support services. (Because) we have concentrated on institutional care, that part of the (health care) network is deficient," she adds.

The United Kingdom has 100 hospices, in which all care is paid for by the National Health Service. The United States has thousands, though only five are non-profit.

Another factor slowing the growth and acceptance of hospices is North America's emphasis on high-technology medical care.

Because of sophisticated methods of treatment, "we are keeping patients with cancer alive longer than before," Dr. Ley says.

Yet acute-care hospitals, which are designed and operated to diagnose, treat and discharge, do not want the dying, she says.

Robert Buckingham, a medical anthropologist who works at the New Haven Hospice in Connecticut, compared hospice care with care on a regular surgical ward in 1976 from the inside.

He spent four days on the surgical ward and four in the palliative care ward. Doctors on regular wards spent an average of 5.5 minutes with each patient, versus 19 in the hospice; nurses spent 2.4 minutes versus 13 minutes.

"You cannot keep these (cancer patients) in institutions until they die," Dr. Ley says. "We (as a society) can't afford it and they don't want to be there."

At its crudest level, she adds, politicians will not respond unless they feel public pressure to do so — and the dying do not count as future voters.

"But their families do, their communities do. The public is increasingly interested in (the hospice movement) and the number of phone calls we get is increasing," she says.

"Hospice care is more than co-ordination of care from a variety of care-givers," Inge Corless, a nurse who worked at St. Peter's Hospice in Albany, N.Y., writes in a textbook on hospice care. "It is scrupulous attention to the physical, psychological, social and spiritual aspects of the patient/family constellation."

Resistance to hospices is still evident in the attitudes of doctors and nurses, who see their roles being usurped, she adds.

Source: *The Globe and Mail,* May 6, 1986.

also involve insomnia, weight loss, and deteriorating health (Vachon, 1979; McPherson, 1983). While in some cultures bereavement is followed by elaborate rituals and dress regulations, many North Americans have dispensed with these rituals and the bereavement often becomes internalized.

The transition from married to single status is usually made with the assistance of family, friends, or widows' support groups. Psychological preparation for the spouse's death or *anticipatory socialization* can assist long-term adjustment and is more possible if friends have been widowed or if the widow is involved in a formalized support group. But psychological adjustment to widowhood is more difficult if there are also financial problems, which are more common for women than for men. Inadequate nutrition, increased alcohol consumption, and declining sanitary conditions at home are more common problems among widowers, but this may be more typical of a generation of men who did not participate in housework and who were socialized to accept segregated marital roles. Decreasing life satisfaction after bereavement is more pronounced for those with poor health, low financial resources, and fewer opportunities to meet new people and be diverted from their grief (Morgan, 1976; Kohn and Kohn, 1979).

Class differences are apparent in the ways in which widows cope with bereavement. Working-class widows tend to become more involved with their children and grandchildren than middle-class widows and are less likely to turn to friends or organizations for assistance and companionship. With less money and fewer personal resources, they experience more loneliness and isolation than the middle class (Lopata, 1973). Similarities between widowed and divorced people have been noted, especially in making the transition from married couple to single person. Research on separation and divorce has suggested that heavy reliance on kin actually makes the transition from married to unmarried status more difficult, even though the financial and child-care assistance may be invaluable to working-class women. Being constantly perceived by relatives as a former wife makes breaking out of this identity more difficult. Finding a job and meeting new people is much easier for those who have a wider and more open social network, which is more typical of the middle classes (Walker, MacBride, and Vachon, 1977).

Widowers experience a higher remarriage rate than widows, partly because men traditionally do the asking and partly because men are socially permitted to marry younger women. This gives men more opportunity than women to remarry. But widowed women have more intimate contacts than widowed men (Strain and Chappell, 1982), which may give women less emotional need to remarry. Widows frequently report little desire to remarry because they feel that they might lose their independence and would be expected to play housekeeper and eventually nurse to their spouse (Lopata, 1970). The argument that marriage as an institution is more advantageous to men than to women should also be considered here. While remarriage rates decrease with age for both sexes, the rates are substantially lower for women.

Various researchers have noted that certain factors make the experience of widowhood more difficult. Since the average age of widowhood is rising (Gee, 1987), women who lose their husbands earlier in life, before their peers do, experience more adjustment problems. Having a low income also makes the experience of widowhood difficult, especially now that the two-income family is becoming more prevalent. Patterns of social support vary considerably in rural and urban areas (Corin, 1987), and rural widows generally are forced to move from the open country to a village or town in order to cope alone (Cape, 1987). Those whose spouse experienced only a brief illness suffer more problems after widowhood because they have had insufficient time to psychologically adjust to their spouse's death. Women report fewer emotional problems after widowhood and report less difficulty than men with living alone, probably because of women's closer ties with relatives and friends. Women, however, suffer a greater financial loss. In conclusion, the transition from married to widowed status generally involves the support of the extended family, but the nature and extent of this support varies by gender and socio-economic status. More longitudinal rather than cross-sectional research is needed to clarify some of this variation but especially to highlight the process of becoming widowed (Matthews, 1987).

CONCLUSION

Although aging is an inevitable physiological process, it can be hastened or decelerated by attitudes, behaviour, and socio-economic conditions. The expectations we have of older people and the opportunities available to them, for example, alter the way they see themselves. The maxim "you are only as old as you feel" may be true, but how we feel is affected not only by our health but by our economic opportunities and the perceived support of others. As we mentioned at the beginning of this chapter, psychological and sociological variables are very much interconnected with physiological aging. This will become more apparent in our discussions of the health status, lifestyle, and attitudes of the elderly in Chapter 3; women and poverty in Chapter 4; and life transitions in Chapter 5.

Throughout the world, the meaning of aging fluctuates with life expectancy and social policies for older people. While a person is considered old in parts of Africa by age forty, North Americans reach sixty-five or seventy before others make this judgment. The socio-economic condition of the elderly has certainly changed in North America, especially since the 1950s. Technological advances have eased the burden of hard physical labour and, through increased productivity, have raised the standard of living for much of the population, including the elderly (Chappell et al., 1986). The process of aging, while partly physiological, varies considerably by culture, social class, and historical time period.

As life expectancy increases in industrialized countries such as Canada and the United States, our definition of "old" rises in chronological age. Improved nutrition, sanitation, and medical care have increased average life expectancies, and social-security programs and retirement policies have accompanied these demographic trends. If mandatory retirement is abolished and considered to be age discrimination, more elderly people may remain in the labour force until they *feel* old or until they choose to retire. At the same time, social and economic policies will have to change to accommodate an older population. In the next chapter we will examine in more detail the issue of population aging and its policy implications for educational and labour force trends, the changing sex ratio and pensions, and the need for expanded facilities for the elderly.

2

THE AGING CANADIAN POPULATION

INTRODUCTION

Since the turn of the century many industrialized countries such as Canada have experienced population aging or an increasing proportion of elderly people in the population. Compared to some European nations, however, Canada's population is still relatively young. While 13.5 percent of France's population, 14.4 percent of Denmark's population, and 16.3 percent of Sweden's population were sixty-five years of age and over in 1981, only 9.7 percent of Canada's population was elderly. The trend of population aging, however, is similar for all Western industrialized countries and Canada has much to learn from observing the European experience. Declining fertility rates and increasing life expectancy are the major reasons for population aging in Canada and other developed countries. But immigration and internal migration have also led to regional pockets of elderly people. Figure 2.1 shows the actual population distribution by age and sex for 1981, as well as future predictions.

DEMOGRAPHIC CHANGES

Reasons for Population Aging

The most important reason for population aging is the decline in the birth rate. Urbanization and industrialization have gradually reduced the benefits of large families and increased child rearing costs; and ideologies promoting high quality child care and improvements in contraceptive technology have lowered birth rates. After the Second World War, birth rates temporarily rose until the mid-1960s during the postwar "baby boom." By the mid-1960s, demand for labour increased in a number of industrialized countries, providing new employment opportunities. More married women were drawn into the labour force because of the shortage of labour and by necessity became increasingly interested in birth control.

FIGURE 2.1

Population by Age and Sex, Canada, 1981 (Census), 2006, and 2031

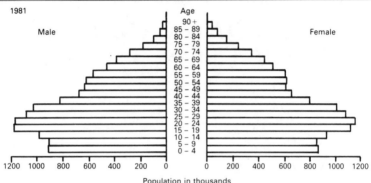

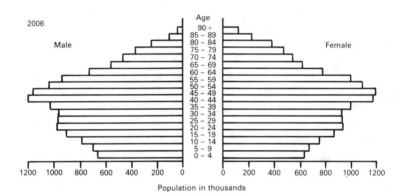

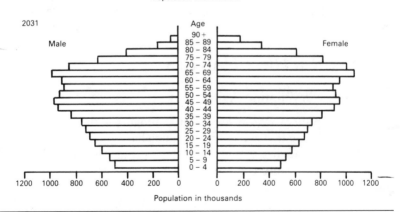

Source: Statistics Canada. *Population Projections for Canada, Provinces and Territories 1984–2006.* Cat. 91–520. Ottawa: Supply and Services, May 1985, p. 49. Reproduced with permission of the Minister of Supply and Services Canada.

TABLE 2.1

Declining Birth Rates in Canada,
1851–1985

Year	Births per 1000 Population
*1851–1861	45
1861–1871	40
1871–1881	37
1881–1891	34
1891–1901	30
1901–1911	31
1911–1921	29
1921	29.3
1931	23.2
1941	22.4
1951	27.2
1961	26.1
1971	16.8
1981	15.3
1985	14.8

* 1851–1921 are estimates

Source: Maureen Baker. *The Family, Changing Trends in Canada*. Toronto: McGraw-Hill Ryerson, 1984, p. 5. Statistics Canada. *Births and Deaths 1985*. Cat. 84–204. Ottawa: November 1986, p. 2.

"The pill" as well as other forms of contraception became widely used in the 1960s, and many women associated paid employment and smaller families with "liberation" from restrictive domestic roles and premature aging.

Canadian birth rates have been falling gradually since the beginning of this century except during the postwar baby boom. In 1921 the crude birth rate was 29.3 per 1000 population, but by 1985 the rate had fallen to 14.8 per 1000 population (Kalbach and McVey, 1979; Statistics Canada, November 1986:2). Table 2.1 shows the trend in the birth rate from 1851 to 1985.

The second major reason for population aging is a rise in life expectancy. Although the average life expectancy at birth may only be forty years in parts of Africa and the Far East, life expectancies in industrialized countries have risen considerably in the last fifty years. This increase resulted mainly from declining rates of infant mortality, deaths during childbirth, and deaths from certain childhood and adult diseases, rather than the expansion of the life span. Improved sanitation, housing, nutrition, and health services were responsible for this decline in mortality.

TABLE 2.2

Average Life Expectancy at Birth
By Sex, Canada, 1931–84

	Male	Female
1931	60.0	62.1
1941	63.0	66.3
1951	66.3	70.8
1961	68.4	74.2
1971	69.3	76.4
1981	71.9	78.9
1984	72.5	79.6

Source: W. Kalbach and W. McVey. *The Demographic Bases of Canadian Society,* 2nd ed. Toronto: McGraw-Hill Ryerson, 1979, p. 72. Statistics Canada. *Population Projections for Canada, Provinces and Territories 1984–2006.* Cat. 91–520. Ottawa: Supply and Services, May 1985, p. 107.

From 1931 to 1984, women's life expectancy at birth increased approximately seventeen years to 79.6 years and men's increased approximately twelve years to 72.5 years as Table 2.2 indicates.

Women generally outlive men by five to eight years in European countries and North America. While there may be biological factors involved in this trend, we also know that men live more dangerous and stressful lives, are more involved in high-risk occupations and hobbies, have higher rates of suicide, smoke more cigarettes, drink more alcohol, and deal with stress in different ways. There is some suggestion that the gender differences may decrease in the future, however, as people live more healthy lifestyles and as occupational hazards lessen (Fries, 1984). Furthermore, the gender differences diminish if we look at life expectancy at age sixty instead of at birth, and by the age of eighty, there is little difference in life expectancies between men and women. The fact that women's life expectancy has increased faster than men's has led to an imbalance in the proportion of elderly women compared to men. Because an increase in the elderly population and especially in elderly women means more people drawing government pensions, these population changes are very significant to public policy.

Also significant to social and health services is the correlation between poverty and lower life expectancy. A recent study by Montreal General Hospital has revealed that people living in the poor Montreal district of Point St. Charles have a life expectancy nine years shorter than their neighbours in nearby Westmount. Residents from Montreal's richest neighbourhoods can also expect about fourteen more years free of disabling health problems than people in the poorest districts. Poor people have above-average rates of malnutrition, high-risk pregnancies, respiratory and cardiovascular disorders, skin diseases, accidents, and mental health problems. The reasons for these class differences are attributed to poor nutrition; low quality accommodation; dangerous jobs; inability to pay for prescriptions and other health aids; and higher rates of smoking, obesity, and physical inactivity among the poor (Regush, 1987).

An aging population has led to important controversies about future patterns of morbidity and mortality, what the maximum potential life span is, and whether there is evidence of a maximum life span being reached in the near future supported by the rectangularization of the survival curve (Kraus, 1987; Simmons-Tropea and Osborn, 1987). We mentioned in Chapter 1 that the rectangularization thesis argues that the probability of death rises sharply at a particular age (over eighty-five), taking on an angular shape on a graph. If morbidity and mortality follow the same pattern in the future, and if the age of the onset of chronic disease rises with the average age of mortality, we may see a similar number of chronically ill older people rather than a significant increase in the future. On the other hand, chronic disease prevalence and disability might increase with rising life expectancy (Gruenberg, 1977; Kramer, 1981; Manton, 1982). Because this debate has implications for future health costs and the planning of services and facilities, it will be discussed further in the section of this chapter on the implications of population aging.

The third major reason for population aging is migration. In developing countries, the migration of young people to the cities to find work is producing over-concentrations of the elderly left behind in villages. Upon retirement, these urban workers often return to their native rural villages. In other parts of the world, especially the Middle East, vast numbers of young people migrate to work in another country, leaving their native land with a disproportionate number of "dependants," including elderly people (United Nations, 1985:17). These trends have serious implications both for social support systems and for the economic development of rural areas.

In developed countries such as the United States and Canada, similar trends in migration of the young to urban areas leave a disproportionate number of elderly people in small rural towns. Besides their physical departure, the loss of young persons of reproductive age causes a decline in fertility, further accelerating the aging process (United Nations, 1985:17). In some developed countries, the preference of older persons to move to warmer climates causes marked concentrations of elderly people in places such as Florida or Victoria, British Columbia. In addition, older people frequently migrate to join their children, especially after the death of their spouse (Auerbach and Gerber, 1976; Longino and Biggar, 1981; Northcott, 1984).

These three factors: a decline in fertility, a rise in life expectancy, and the migration of young workers as well as older people lead to population aging. But the most influential of these three factors is a decline in fertility (United Nations, 1985:14).

The high birth rate after the Second World War led to a temporary focus on the needs of young people in North America. But now this cohort of baby-boomers is approaching middle age. To coincide with their consumer needs and interests, advertisers and business people are beginning to change their marketing strategies and products to cater to an older population. Scarce social resources are being reallocated to policies and programs for older people. At the same time, connotations of "old" and "young" are changing with the demographic trend to an older population.

Dependency Ratios

When setting priorities for social programs such as the planning of schools or hospitals, or predicting the future viability of pension plans, social planners and policy-makers need some indication of the growth of certain sectors of the population. Dependency ratios have been used to make rough comparisons between the productive and non-productive sectors of the population. The age groups usually assumed to be dependent or non-productive are under twenty years old and over sixty-four years old, but they vary in different countries. The productive years in Canada are usually assumed to be from twenty to sixty-four years of age, but these age groups are only approximations of dependence and productivity, as 7 percent of those aged sixty-five and over are still working for pay and one quarter of those aged twenty to sixty-four are not (Statistics Canada, January 1986:26).

While the dependency ratio for children has been declining in Canada since the mid-1960s, the ratio for the elderly has increased from 8.8 per 100 "productive" people in 1911 to 18.4 per 100 in 1984 and is expected to rise to about 33 per 100 in 2031 (National Council of Welfare, 1984b:21). If birth rates remain low, the total dependency ratios may drop considerably to reach a low point in 2011 and then rise to the 1971 level in 2031, as Table 2.3 and Figure 2.2 indicate. But total dependency ratios will still be far below the 1961 level at all points in the foreseeable future. In other words, the labour force will be larger in the future because the decline in the birth rate has been faster than the rise in the elderly population. This suggests that there will be no "crisis" associated with the aging population (Denton, Feaver, and Spencer, 1987).

Different levels of economic development, immigration, and internal migration have led to varying provincial and regional dependency ratios in Canada. For example, Saskatchewan has lost many young people in recent years as agricultural profits have fallen and young people have

TABLE 2.3

Dependency Ratios*, According to the Low-growth Scenario, Canada 1971–2031

	Dependency Ratio		
Year	Child (0–17)	Old (65 +)	Total
1971	63.4	14.4	77.8
1981	45.2	15.6	60.8
1991	37.1	21.6	58.7
2001	30.9	24.4	55.2
2011	25.3	27.4	52.7
2021	25.2	37.8	63.0
2031	25.0	51.6	76.6

* The number of people of "dependent ages" per 100 persons of "working age."

Source: Statistics Canada. *Population Projections for Canada, Provinces and Territories, 1984–2006*. Cat. 91–520. Ottawa: Supply and Services, May 1985, p. 55.

moved to other provinces for higher education and jobs. Retired people often move from both farms and large cities to towns, leaving small communities across Canada with high elderly dependency ratios (Hodge and Qadeer, 1983:37). Suburban areas that expanded in the 1950s such as parts of Toronto and Montreal are also experiencing the aging of their population.

When observing trends in dependency ratios it is necessary to look at children and the elderly separately. Otherwise, the effect of a reduction in the child population may be cancelled out by an increase in the proportion of elderly people. Although this would leave the relative size of the working population stable, it would have different implications for governments and social services. While many of the costs of child rearing and child care are paid for by the family, support of the elderly is financed largely by the state, especially the federal government, in the form of public pensions.

Dependency ratios have been criticized for implying that the per capita cost of supporting "dependants" is the same for all age groups (Crown, 1985). In Canada the cost of social-security payments and health care for older people is much higher than similar benefits for children. Education is a major expense for both provincial and federal governments, but with an aging population, social-security costs will rise considerably while education costs will probably decline (Foot, 1982; Messinger and

FIGURE 2.2

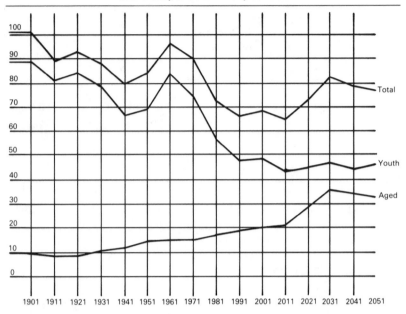

Dependency Ratios for Aged, Youth*, and Total, 1901 to 1981, Canada

* Youth is considered to be under 20 years old.

Source: National Council of Welfare. *Sixty-five and Older.* Ottawa: 1984, p. 22a.

Powell, 1987). However, we cannot just look at dependency ratios and extrapolations from demographic statistics when we predict future social spending. Political and economic decisions are also important. Some authors have argued that public payments for children are an investment in future productivity while payments to the elderly are just "maintenance" (Clark and Spengler, 1978). Yet considering that most older people have spent their adult lives in "productive" activities, either as part of the labour force or producing and rearing the next generation, society can ill afford to neglect them in their old age. In addition, it is certainly clear that not all people aged sixty-five and over are "dependants"; a word with pejorative connotations. Some are still working for pay or living on their investments. Others may be lending money to their children to assist with their mortgages, providing important services such as babysitting, or performing essential work as volunteers. The fact remains, however, that a high proportion of elderly people in the population means higher social-security costs for the federal government. We will examine the implications of this trend in more detail in Chapter 4.

CANADA'S AGE STRUCTURE COMPARED TO OTHER NATIONS

Although similar demographic trends have occurred in other industrialized nations, the process of aging has been slower in Canada. A number of factors have slowed this process. Firstly, large-scale immigration has always supplemented Canada's population and those entering this country have usually been young people with marketable skills. These immigrants often brought their spouses to Canada, but immigrant families have generally produced fewer children than native-born families. Accepting large numbers of immigrants each year has kept the average age in this country relatively low.

Secondly, the proportion of rural dwellers has been higher in Canada than in some European countries. Rural residence has been associated with higher birth rates because children's labour is useful on the farm, overcrowding is not a problem, and living costs are lower (Kalbach and McVey, 1979:101; Gaffield, 1984).

Thirdly, a large Catholic population, especially among the French and native people, has until recently been associated with high birth rates. Although fertility has declined dramatically in Quebec, birth rates are still high for native people, particularly status Indians on reserves and Inuits in the North.

Canada also lost fewer young men during the Second World War than countries such as Germany and Russia. Loss of young men reduced the marriage rate and subsequent birth rate in these countries.

These factors have led to higher dependency ratios for children in Canada compared to some European nations such as Germany and Great Britain, and account for the delay in our population aging.

The United Nations gathers statistics on the age distribution in various countries. In many parts of the world, the age at which a child is considered to be an adult is fifteen years. The lack of higher education and the need for young people to contribute to the family income in developing countries mean that the period we call "adolescence" is virtually non-existent or at best truncated, especially among the poor. Since life expectancies at birth are much lower in developing countries, age sixty is considered "elderly."

The age groups 0 to 14 and 60 and Over are calculated as percentages of total population figures for selected countries and shown in Table 2.4. These figures clearly illustrate that developing countries tend to have more children and fewer elderly, while developed countries tend to have fewer children and more elderly. The life expectancy differences between men and women are greater in the industrialized or developed countries, but few differences exist in developing nations where rates of maternal death and infant mortality are relatively high.

TABLE 2.4

Age Groups 0 to 14 and 60 and Over as a Percentage of Total Population in Selected Countries, 1980

	Age Group 0-14	Age Group 60+	
		Male	Female
Australia	25.6%	11.9%	14.8%
Bangladesh	45.8	4.3	4.3
Belgium	20.1	15.7	20.7
Canada	23.2	11.5	14.0
China	33.6	7.9	8.9
Cuba	31.3	10.6	10.3
Denmark	20.9	17.3	21.4
Ethiopia	45.1	4.0	4.5
France	22.2	14.1	19.8
Federal Republic of Germany	18.6	14.4	22.6
India	40.1	5.0	4.9
Italy	21.7	15.5	19.6
Japan	23.4	11.1	14.3
Mexico	44.6	4.7	5.6
Norway	22.2	17.9	22.3
Pakistan	45.0	4.8	4.5
Poland	24.1	10.8	15.3
Sweden	19.6	19.9	23.9
United Kingdom (Britain & N. Ireland)	20.8	17.2	22.6
U.S.A.	22.9	13.3	17.0

Source: Extracted from United Nations. *World Statistics in Brief.* New York: 1983. Copyright, United Nations (1983). Reproduced by permission.

Although most of the research on population aging has been done in industrialized countries, international organizations such as the United Nations are recognizing that population aging is also taking place in the Third World. Because of the larger populations in countries such as China and India, the number of elderly people is growing faster than in industrialized countries and will lead eventually to more elderly people living in the Third World than in developed countries. Population aging is particularly an issue in rural areas because young people leave to find work in the cities, but it is also a problem in urban centres. Urban areas attract and retain more older females than males, and older females are more likely to find themselves poor and dependent because of their previous work lives and family obligations (Neysmith and Edwardh, 1984).

In countries with low birth rates and high life expectancies, the aging population has had numerous implications for education, labour force participation, health care, and pensions. Countries such as Sweden, where almost one quarter of the women and one fifth of the men are over sixty years old, must alter all their social institutions and services to accommodate a growing elderly population. In the next section we will look at some of the implications of the aging Canadian population in more detail.

IMPLICATIONS OF AN AGING POPULATION

Educational Trends and the Aging Labour Force

During the 1960s, new employment opportunities were created when bureaucracies expanded, school boards hired new staff to accommodate the baby-boom generation, and the service sector of the economy grew. The post-secondary education system expanded to train more specialists for the labour market and to meet the educational needs of the larger proportions of young people who might otherwise have been unemployed. An increasing percentage of young people began to attend college and university during the 1960s and 1970s. While 6 percent of eighteen to twenty-four-year-olds attended post-secondary institutions in 1951, this figure rose to 22 percent in 1983 (Statistics Canada, 1980;1984). More women entered colleges and universities, and young people from poorer families took advantage of the student loans and grants to further their education. Many of these graduates entered the labour force in the early 1970s, but towards the end of that decade the economy took a downturn and jobs became more scarce.

As birth rates fell in the 1960s, the decline in the school-aged population began to affect educational funding policies and empty elementary school classrooms started being used for community activities. The hiring of teachers was curtailed, especially by the late 1970s. When university enrolment appeared to be threatened by the aging population, administrators sought new target populations and found them in middle-aged women and senior citizens. Some universities offered free tuition for seniors, but no real attempt was made to accommodate older students into university life, perhaps because these students were not viewed as future "investments" in the way that youth often are (Myles and Boyd, 1982).

While those with advanced education have been able to find work more easily, particularly since the Second World War, graduates began to have increased difficulty finding work in their field of specialization in the late 1970s. Unemployment rates rose faster for school drop-outs, but graduates also experienced difficulty breaking into the permanent labour force. Employers are now more likely to hire on a temporary basis in case they need to cut personnel costs in the near future. Short-term contractual appointments not only give them greater flexibility but also

Middle-age spread on campus

Greying professors higher education's gravest problem?

From the early 1960s to the early 1980s, full-time university professors in Canada increased from about 10,000 to more than 33,000, keeping pace with the extraordinary expansion of all post-secondary institutions. From 1964 to 1972, the peak growth years, faculty ballooned by more than 2,000 new positions yearly. And since Canada had not produced anywhere near enough PhDs to fill all those jobs, our universities recruited feverishly from abroad, from Britain, from Europe and Australia, above all from the United States.

Then the boom ended. Drastically shrinking budgets and steady-state or declining enrolments have meant that most university departments have been frozen for at least six years. And because such large numbers of faculty were hired in such a short space of time, the senior common rooms of the nation are peopled almost exclusively now by academics between the ages of 35 and 54. Three-quarters of Canadian professors are bunched in that age group. Three problems arise from this unique situation: higher costs, intellectual stagnation and the potential loss of an academic generation.

This year, 76 per cent of university teachers are at a rank of full or associate professor, with an average salary of $53,000. Assistants and lecturers, who average $33,000, make up only 23 per cent of the teaching staff. By 1990, the higher-paid ranks will be up to 81 per cent of the total. Universities are finding that more and more of their dwindling budgets are going into professorial salaries each year, with no quantifiable increase in excellence or productivity.

In a few disciplines, notably mathematics and pure sciences, academics often do their most creative work when they are very young. But generally speaking, it would be knee-jerk agism to say that younger is better. What younger teachers do provide, apart from lower costs, is the mix of attitudes that should be a sine qua non of university life and which is sorely lacking on Canadian campuses today. At the moment, it's a Big Chill faculty talking to a Breakfast Club student body and the dialogue is getting more and more attenuated.

The most serious problem generated by these odd faculty demographics is the potential loss of a generation of Canadian scholars. For the first time in our history, we are producing a surplus of Canadian PhDs, and what a surplus: about seven times more than can possibly expect to get university teaching positions in the next decade. The majority of them, faced with a hopelessly plugged-up

system, are abandoning the pursuit of academic careers. The ones who won't give up become scholar gypsies, roaming from campus to campus, lurching from a one-year appointment here to two years there, but never being admitted to the tenure stream that ensures career continuity.

If the university were a constantly diminishing organism, this reduction of new talent to a trickle would be cause for only mild concern. But that isn't the case. About 10 years from now, in the late nineties, the baby boomlet (the children of the baby boomers) will start to swell university enrolments again, just when the huge cohort of present faculty start retiring — at the rate of 2,000 a year, just the way they were hired. But by then, after 15 years of disastrous job prospects, where will we find the academic talent to cope with a new generation of students? We could be right back where we were in the mid-sixties, with a drastic national shortage of university teachers.

Bronwyn Drainie is a Toronto writer and broadcaster. With permission.

save money on benefits such as pension contributions. Many part-time and temporary workers are not covered by the same labour legislation and collective agreements as full-time workers, but they are expected to work as hard and are often more productive.

For those hired in permanent jobs in the 1970s and 1980s, promotional possibilities are now limited because of the large number of employees hired during those decades who will not retire for many years. Bureaucracies such as the civil service and universities have become top-heavy with too many middle- and higher-level employees, and more of the dwindling budgets of universities are going into professorial salaries each year (Drainie, 1986). Blocked mobility is becoming a serious problem in occupations with life-time career ladders. People have to wait years for promotion regardless of merit and vacancies are scarce because few employers are hiring. In some organizations job security for those with seniority is written into union contracts, preventing even the less competent from being fired. Yet well-qualified young people remain unemployed or marginally employed. With few chances for advancement, some young professionals are becoming disgruntled and are turning to unions to protect their jobs, improve the quality of their working environment, or review the productivity and job security of their older colleagues. Others are becoming more competitive and cut-throat in their attempts to be promoted. Productivity by young people in marginal jobs, however, may actually increase because they have to work harder than their predecessors to find permanence in the hierarchy.

Throughout this discussion, we must keep in mind that career mobility has been historically available mainly to white-collar men. The occupational mobility of blue-collar and immigrant men and many women was generally blocked by lack of promotional opportunities in dead-end jobs and by discriminatory attitudes. The aging population, therefore, may have greater consequences for the relatively privileged group that used to have a clear career path than for certain minority groups (McDaniel, 1985). Economic cutbacks and technological change, however, may have serious consequences for those who have historically experienced employment discrimination and high rates of unemployment.

Contractual employees may be caught for years without the security of continuing work or future pensions. Between jobs they must rely on government assistance or their savings, or somehow create work through self-employment. Conflict theorists would argue that relations between the permanently employed and the marginally employed are bound to become antagonistic if the gap between them grows wider. This potential problem could be dramatically improved through policy changes, however, for the structure of work could accommodate an aging work force and at the same time enable young people to enter the job market. New jobs could be created by reducing the work week, restricting people from working overtime, and sharing work or jobs among more people. Sabbaticals or occupational renewal leaves could create a permanent need for temporary replacements, but temporary and part-time workers would have to receive comparable fringe benefits on a prorated basis. More flexible work hours, programs of gradual retirement, and major changes to pension plans could also assist older workers, and the trend towards early retirement might create more jobs as well. Many of these modifications to the structure of work would have little cost but would require the political will to fight against existing vested interests. Rules qualifying people for pensions would have to be relaxed as well if gradual retirement and worksharing were introduced.

The Changing Sex Ratio and Pensions

Because women's life expectancy has increased faster than men's in industrialized societies, a larger proportion of the elderly are female. This is particularly true among the older elderly as Figure 2.3 indicates. In 1921 less than half the Canadian population aged sixty-five and over were women. In 1981, 57 percent of Canadians aged sixty-five and over and 62 percent of those aged seventy-five and over were female. If present trends continue, 60 percent of those aged sixty-five and over and 66 percent of those aged seventy-five and over will be women by 2001 (National Council on Welfare, 1984b:8). The rising percentage of women among the elderly is particularly significant when we realize that many

FIGURE 2.3

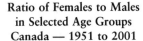

**Ratio of Females to Males
in Selected Age Groups
Canada — 1951 to 2001**

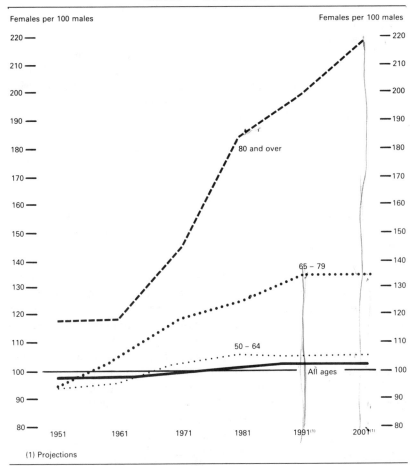

(1) Projections

Source: Health and Welfare Canada. *Fact Book on Aging in Canada*. Ottawa:
          1983, p. 21. Reproduced with permission of the Minister of Supply
          and Services Canada.

women have been financially dependent throughout their lives and are
poorer than men in their old age.

Many married women outlive their husbands by five to ten years
because they tend to marry older men and their life expectancies are
longer. In 1981 only 14 percent of men aged sixty-five and over were

widowed compared to 49 percent of women (National Council of Welfare, 1984b:14). After assuming that their husbands would look after them financially, many elderly women have discovered that the death of their husband has left them with little money, since many private pensions do not have survivor's benefits. Consequently numerous widows must depend on government pensions such as Old Age Security and the Guaranteed Income Supplement.

Women who worked for pay most of their lives likely earned lower wages than men, and since work-related pensions are based on contributions from pay-cheques, lower pay-cheques mean lower pensions. Prior to the mid-1970s, the retirement age for women was often five years earlier than for men. While this may have coincided with some women's preference to retire at the same time as their (older) husband, it decreased women's retirement benefits relative to men's. Considering the longer life expectancy for women, their retirement age should have been *older* than men's, if not the same. Moreover, many women have no employer pension at all because they were encouraged to leave the labour force to have children and in the absence of public day care had to stay home to raise them. Others worked part-time or in temporary positions and therefore did not qualify for pension plan membership. Consequently many retired women must rely on public support or their meagre savings.

The financial dependence of many elderly women is augmented by lower levels of formal education than men of the same cohort. While this often translates into lower income, it may also be synonymous with lower levels of confidence in their own abilities to cope with the practical aspects of life, especially investments, taxes, and planning for the future. Older women have often been encouraged to accept passive and domestic roles and to wait for others to take the initiative and show them the way. This can impede coping with widowhood, particularly in developing new relationships, investing money wisely, or filling lonely hours. Unusual personal assertiveness is required to overcome a lifetime of financial and emotional dependency and social expectations of passivity outside the domestic sphere. Moreover, the experience of living alone, which has increased among widows as well as for people of all age groups, necessitates greater independence than many women are prepared for.

The poverty of older women will undoubtedly be reduced as more women enter permanent jobs with employer-sponsored pensions and Canada Pension Plan membership. Yet fewer younger women are enrolled in pension plans than are men of the same age, and women are still encouraged to work part-time or in temporary jobs without employer pension plans or to take time out of the labour force to care for their children. Furthermore, employers are still permitted to provide no pension plan. But even when women are enrolled in pension plans their contributions are lower because their incomes are lower. So while future elderly women will be better educated and less likely to be caught without

The rocky road to homemaker pensions

With his new proposal to include homemakers in the Canada Pension Plan, Welfare Minister Jake Epp has raised one of the touchiest issues on the social policy agenda. It has flummoxed federal and provincial governments for years.

Epp has not disclosed details of his plan, submitted to his provincial counterparts this week. But reports claim it would provide housewives with a CPP (or Quebec Plan) pension of about half the maximum allowed to current participants. Contributions would also be half the maximum, with government subsidies for low-income homemakers.

The intention is unassailable: to provide income security for women who cannot participate in the CPP or company pensions because they do not "earn income" of their own. The need is equally obvious, because women form a disproportionate part of the elderly poor in this country.

But adding a homemaker's benefit to the CPP has caused no end of political controversy. The Liberal government rejected the concept in a green paper in 1982. It argued instead for new "pension-splitting" provisions to assure widows and divorcees a bigger share of a spouse's earned benefits.

In 1983, a special all-party Commons committee saw things differently — endorsing a homemakers' pension as well as a better pension-splitting system.

Several provinces have opposed housewife pensions in the past. Opponents have sometimes argued that pensions are meant to replace earnings; where there are no earnings to begin with, there is nothing to compensate for. Another issue is cost.

In fact, financing the whole Canada Pension Plan remains one of the prickliest nettles for Parliament and the provinces (two-thirds of which must approve any CPP amendment). At its inception in 1966, the plan was designed to be "partially funded," meaning that contributions from employees and employers do not pay the total cost. Over the years it has built up surpluses. But as more people become beneficiaries, contributions must increase.

Raising contributions is something no politician relishes. Because it is backed by federal and provincial governments, the CPP literally cannot go bankrupt. But even governments cannot defy the nation's aging demography. Either CPP premiums rise, or the treasury must stand ready with subsidies. Neither course is politically easy.

Courtesy of *The Ottawa Citizen*, September 20, 1985.

The experience of living alone necessitates greater independence than many women are prepared for. (Public Archives Canada/PA 93924)

savings or pension benefits than today's elderly women, the problem will not dissipate without further policy reform.

Changes to the status of all women may lessen the "pension burden" for the state and the poverty of older women. Equal pay for work of equal value, public day care, equal benefits for part-time employees, pensions for homemakers, a more equal division of labour in the home between husbands and wives, and major improvements to the Canada Pension Plan are all necessary to reduce the poverty of elderly women. Poverty in old age is often the result of a lifetime of discriminatory treatment or lower status. This is certainly the case with women.

The Need for Expanded Facilities for the Elderly

The aging Canadian population necessitates an expansion of social services, pension funds, housing, and consumer products favoured by the elderly. During a recession, however, expanding services is financially and politically difficult. Governments around the world, for example, are trying to find ways of reducing medical and hospital costs while improving health service for the elderly.

Increasing age is now associated with chronic illness and physical health dysfunction and an aging population will need better chronic rather than acute health care (Brunet, 1985). As a group, the elderly use more medical facilities than any other adult age group — the "old elderly" more than the "young elderly" and women more than men (Martin, 1982). The older population, however, is highly differentiated in health status and in consequent need for services. Some categories of older people are healthier than others, and some require hospital care more than others. Furthermore, perceptions of health needs may vary by cultural group. In reality, a small minority of very old people are using the majority of health resources (Shapiro and Roos, 1987) such as acute hospital care, expensive life-prolonging machines, and medical specialists. Most older Canadians, however, spend little time in either acute- or chronic-care hospitals. Several authors have suggested that major reforms rather than expansion are needed in the health-care system to focus more on prevention, community and home care, and the use of a variety of health practitioners (Evans, 1984; Chappell et al., 1986). In fact, an aging population may not necessitate an expansion of present medical services at all because the age of the onset of chronic illness might rise with more healthy lifestyles and medical breakthroughs. Reforms in the entire health-care system, however, may help reduce health-care costs and better serve an older population.

A major controversy in the research exists over future predictions of illness and life expectancy. Fries (1984) has argued that the average age at which older people become chronically ill has been extended by more healthy lifestyles, improved diet, exercise, and medical breakthroughs. But the life span has not substantially increased for older people and, Fries has argued, we are fast approaching its natural limits. This means that morbidity or illness will be compressed into fewer years and into a smaller proportion of the life span. If this "compression of morbidity" hypothesis is valid, there will be no "geriatric crisis" in the future. Health costs will not rise significantly and we will not see a larger proportion of elderly people in nursing homes or chronic-care institutions.

The compression of morbidity hypothesis has been criticized, however, for placing too much faith on the value of preventative medicine, for drawing attention away from the successes of biomedical science, for assuming that the life span will not increase, and for ignoring past trends in the age of the onset of disability, which has not been rising significantly (Schneider and Brody, 1983). If doctors continue to use medical technology and dramatic operations to combat death, then morbidity could actually increase as death is prolonged. This would mean that medical costs would continue to rise. Similarly, if there is no sizable investment in preventative health care or reduction of environmental pollution, the onset of morbidity or chronic illness will not change. Although Fries is aware of these social and political variables affecting the compression of morbidity hypothesis, he is optimistic that the age of the onset of chronic illness will rise and that medical costs will decline in the future. In a recent article based on American and Canadian statistics, Arthur Kraus (1987) argues that the usual life span increased by at least two years in the period from 1960–1980 in North America. Kraus defines "usual life span" as the age to which 1.0 percent of a cohort would survive. These data contradict Fries' assumptions of the compression of morbidity hypothesis.

Simmons-Tropea and Osborn (1987) present Canadian evidence of an increasing level of short-term and long-term disability with age for both sexes from 1951 to 1978. They argue that non-lethal causes of disability such as arthritis, rheumatism, and mental disability will continue, but causes of death such as cardiovascular disease may be subject to control. Improvements in mortality depend on a number of social, political, and medical factors, including advances in research regarding disease etiology, development of new diagnostic and surgical techniques, the presence of environmental pollutants, the incidence of violence, and improvements in lifestyle (Rice and Feldman, 1983:362).

One fact that is disturbing to health-care planners is the apparent higher levels of institutionalization of the elderly in Canada compared to European nations such as Great Britain, France, and Sweden, although this may largely be a result of how statistics are calculated (Chappell et al., 1986). The need for inducements to help the elderly stay out of hospitals and nursing homes wherever possible has been reiterated in many Canadian government documents. The practice in European countries of providing services and subsidies for the elderly to remain in their own homes and of paying family members to care for their elderly at home appears to save public money. Although the move away from institutionalization is largely based on economic feasibility, it also has a humanistic motive, since elderly people living at home express greater life satisfaction than those in institutions (Connidis, 1985). But families are already providing home care, and whether or not the extent of support can be augmented is debatable.

While the family remains the basis of emotional ties and mutual support throughout the world, the demographic changes we have outlined will increasingly limit the family's capacity to continue its care-giving role. Firstly, lower fertility rates and smaller families will leave fewer children available to care for aging parents. Secondly, increased life expectancies could lead to larger numbers of very old people requiring intensive nursing, which would also tax the resources of families as care-providers. However, this scenario has been seriously questioned by those who foresee a more healthy older population in the future (Marshall, 1981; Fries, 1984). It is becoming increasingly possible that middle-aged people could have parents and grandparents still alive and be responsible for them as well as their own children and even grandchildren. Thirdly, out-migration of the young also acts to weaken family support available to older persons left behind (United Nations, 1985:73,74). Similarly, the re-entrance of many middle-aged women into the labour force implies that although they have traditionally been the major care-givers of older parents, they may not have as much time for this activity as they used to in the past.

Governments have become increasingly involved in programs for the elderly, especially since the 1950s. The Canadian federal government provides income support programs and income tax exemptions and subsidizes cultural, recreational, and housing projects. The National Advisory Council on Aging counsels the Minister of Health and Welfare and stimulates public discussion on matters relating to the quality of life of the elderly. The Canada Assistance Plan administered by Health and Welfare Canada shares with the provinces the cost of assistance to persons in need. For the elderly, this may include food, shelter, clothing, transportation, or institutional care. The federal Medicare plan covers medical and health services, but the provinces are responsible for administering their own social and health programs. Some examples of provincial services for the elderly include day-care programs, senior citizens' drug plans, extended-care hospitals, transportation services, and seniors' community centres. Many of these programs will have to expand or change to meet the increasing numbers of elderly people in the Canadian population, and new policies will have to be negotiated.

The aging of the Canadian population will require careful planning for the future, but it is by no means the "crisis" portrayed by the media and some organizations catering to the elderly. Furthermore, portraying the aging population as a crisis situation may actually be a political strategy to generate increased public support for funding hospitals, nursing homes, or private pension plans (Denton, Li, and Spencer, 1987). Banks and trust companies can certainly profit by encouraging people to save for their future with RRSPs by leading them to believe that public pensions such as the Canada Pension Plan are nearing bankruptcy. Health care and pension costs will certainly increase in the future, but the demographic changes necessitating this rise will occur gradually to allow for adaptation. At the same time, other public expenses such as education will probably fall with declining fertility (Messinger and Powell, 1987).

Some private companies have already attempted to capture the growing seniors' market by offering discounts to those aged sixty-five and over. This is good public relations but it also increases profits. The retail clothing industry is showing more older people as models in the fashion pages of newspapers and magazines. Travel companies are moving in on the seniors' market for cruises, holiday resorts, and special package tours. Business people as well as governments are adapting their strategies and policies for an aging population and the accuracy of demographic predictions could be very consequential.

CONCLUSION

Public concern about the aging population is not a new phenomenon in Canada. During the 1930s when birth rates fell rapidly, demographers and policy-makers became concerned about the implications of population aging. But after World War II when birth rates rose again, the practical problems of dealing with so many children became a more important policy issue. Although many industrialized countries are now expanding services and facilities for the elderly, the dramatic increase in the proportion of elderly people is not a permanent trend but is largely a result of the postwar baby boom. Assuming that the birth rate remains low, the baby-boom generation will have reached the end of its life span by 2031, and the age distribution of the population will gradually become more evenly distributed after that date.

By the time the "baby-boomers" reach retirement age, "grey power" will likely increase. If mandatory retirement is outlawed under the Charter of Rights, older people may continue to occupy powerful positions in politics and in the labour force. In addition, future experiences with aging will be different because young adults today generally have more education and enjoy more employment and social-security benefits. Attitudes about the needs and capabilities of the elderly undoubtedly will change as employer-sponsored pensions become more widespread, families become smaller, marriages become less permanent, living alone becomes more acceptable, and a larger proportion of the population becomes elderly. If life expectancies continue to rise, our definitions of *old* will also have to be upgraded.

Some authors have suggested that the aging population of Canada will encourage intergenerational conflict between the young who are competing for jobs and resources and the older citizens who are holding on to their jobs. But the real conflict will more likely occur between groups that have catered to the needs of or benefitted from a youthful population and those whose interests lie with the elderly (Myles, 1982). For example, the schools and universities that grew and based their funding policies on large numbers of students will fight to change the funding formulas when they are no longer to their advantage. Many of our social organizations have been designed for a youthful population, and changing them will create more conflict between administrators than we will see between the generations. After all, the young and middle-aged have a self-interest in improving pensions and benefits for the elderly. If pensions are inadequate, the elderly will stay in the labour force and block mobility channels for the young. Improved conditions for the elderly will eventually benefit all individuals in the community but not all organizations.

In the next chapter we will examine changes to the economic, employment, and health status of elderly people with industrialization and population aging. While the focus of the chapter is on Canada, we also will look at cross-cultural research from preliterate and other industrialized societies. The central question in these studies relates to which economic, demographic, and political conditions improve or deteriorate the status of the elderly over time.

3

THE CHANGING STATUS
OF THE ELDERLY

INTRODUCTION

The status and situation of the elderly in Western industrialized societies have changed considerably since the nineteenth century. Firstly, the elderly used to form a smaller segment of the population and consequently had less social visibility and political clout. In 1901 only 5 percent of the Canadian population was aged sixty-five and over, but by 1981 this figure had risen to 10 percent (Statistics Canada, April 1984). By the year 2031, some demographers predict that 20 percent of the Canadian population will be elderly (Martin, 1982:147). Lower birth rates, certain immigration patterns, and longer life expectancies have increased the elderly population. As the proportion of elderly people grows, their visibility increases, their concerns about pensions and health care become important topics of social debate, and they consequently gain political power.

Secondly, the development of retirement and pension benefits have substantially raised the economic status of the elderly relative to other age groups. In 1969, for example, 41.4 percent of Canadian families headed by elders were below the Statistics Canada poverty line, but by 1982 the rate had fallen to 11.7 percent. These low-income families headed by elders constituted 26 percent of all poor families in 1969, but only 10.7 percent in 1982 (National Council of Welfare, 1984b:33).

Men and women used to work until they were physically incapable because there were no government or employer-sponsored pensions, no medical or accident insurance policies, and no subsidized apartments for senior citizens. Older people without savings hoped their adult children would look after them. Otherwise, they could look forward to the "poor house," some assistance from the community, or help from a charitable organization. Having several children was seen as "insurance" for old age, and elderly parents hoped that their children would continue the family farm or business and live with or near them. Those privileged elderly who had money could hire housekeepers, live-in companions, nurses, or private doctors. But most older people relied on their own financial resources or those of their family, neighbours, or church. Benevolent societies and church groups often collected money to pay for funerals or to help out widows. Parents who were widowed were sometimes forced to break up the family and have some of their young children cared for by others.

Before government pensions, very few employers provided their own retirement plans. People were generally expected to save for their old age or work until they died. Young male employees assumed that they would start at the bottom of the hierarchy and gradually work their way up over time. The principles of seniority and hard work were expected to allow people to improve their financial position as they aged. For women, marriage was usually seen as essential for financial security and married women with children expected to be supported by their husbands in return for unpaid domestic work. Many women assumed that if their deceased husbands left inadequate savings, their children could be relied on to care for them in their old age. Since the family was expected to look after its members, governments only intervened when the family clearly could not provide assistance to the poor or elderly.

It was not until 1927 that the Canadian government provided cost-sharing with the provinces for an old-age pension, but it was initially available only to those seventy years old and over who had low incomes. Since the 1960s Canadian federal and provincial governments have dramatically improved pensions as well as medical and social services as we shall see in Chapter 4. Most of these programs assist those with lower incomes, but others provide medical, housing, or recreational services. Government benefits have substantially contributed to the financial well-being of the elderly and enabled them to maintain some independence from their family. This intervention has changed both the status of the elderly compared to other groups and the attitudes about aging. For example, people fear the aging process and retirement less if they are financially secure and know they can afford access to medical services (McPherson, 1983:387). Yet the improved financial position of the elderly has increased their dependency on the state (Walker, 1983).

In countries less developed than Canada, however, governments have not been able to offer many social-security or income-support programs to anyone, let alone the elderly. For the majority of people in Third World countries, poverty and hunger are widespread, social and health services are underdeveloped, and life expectancies at birth are relatively low. Yet for those who survive past middle age, life expectancy is closer to that of developed countries. Without social-security programs, however, the elderly must work until disabled and then rely on their families or friends for assistance. As in industrialized countries, life expectancies are higher for the rich, but the quality of life is more closely related to family resources than in countries with income-support programs.

With industrialization and urbanization, traditional skills and experience have become less important. (Public Archives Canada/PA 43644)

THE EFFECT OF INDUSTRIALIZATION ON THE ELDERLY

Despite recent improvements to elderly people's incomes in industrialized countries, some researchers have suggested that the status of the elderly has generally fallen with modernization and industrialization (Cowgill and Holmes, 1972). The modernization thesis suggests that in preliterate societies young people had to rely on the memory, skills, and experience of older people and that those with specialized knowledge passed on their expertise to the young. Older men have generally held the highest political and religious positions, but with industrialization and urbanization, traditional skills and experience have become less important than higher education, flexibility, and technical expertise. Young people often move away from home, acquire more formal education than their parents, and follow employment opportunities. Consequently many young people now have less in common with older people and may feel that they have less to learn from them.

The modernization theory states that with industrialization, achievement often becomes more important than tradition or even seniority. Educated young people expect to enter the labour force somewhere in the middle of the hierarchy rather than at the bottom. They expect to be promoted by merit rather than by age or seniority and hope to share responsibility with older people, to gain prestige, and to earn higher incomes than those with less education. Older people with outdated skills are edged out of important jobs or the labour market itself. Respecting one's elders becomes a matter of decision rather than tradition, and if the older person is admirable or very skillful, he or she commands respect. In other words, some researchers have claimed that technological change and higher education have lowered the status of the elderly (Maxwell and Silverman, 1970; Cowgill and Holmes, 1972).

Other researchers have argued that the relationship between modernization and the status of the elderly is curvilinear rather than simply linear (Palmore and Manton, 1974). Although status may fall in the early stages of industrialization when the birth rate generally increases, with advanced industrialization the status of the elderly begins to rise again. As the elderly begin to form a larger segment of the population, they are able to command more political clout. Concern about the welfare of the elderly leads to government programs to supplement their income, subsidize their expenses, and increase their life satisfaction. Policies such as mandatory retirement may be challenged along with previous assumptions about the abilities and preferred lifestyle of the elderly.

Not everyone agrees, however, that the status of the elderly was actually higher in preliterate society than in the early stages of industrial society (Holmberg, 1969:224–225; Fischer, 1977). In preliterate societies in which hunting, warfare, or physical prowess were important, elderly men lost status when their physical strength and endurance faded. Elderly women may have gained status as they aged, from producing children and successfully rearing them, but after their children were grown and they no longer had the strength to gather food, their status often declined.

Part of this controversy has been resolved by analysing different types of preliterate societies. Anthropologists and sociologists have generally concluded that high status for the elderly was prevalent in sedentary rather than nomadic societies. With a food surplus, the elderly enjoyed an adequate diet, but during a food shortage, older people were pressured to allow children a greater share of food. Where cultural values assigned religious, educational, social, and political leadership roles to the elderly, as with the Anicinabe of the Georgian Bay area of Ontario (Vanderburgh, 1987), they have maintained high status. The elderly have also been able to maintain or gain higher status with increasing age when they controlled property or wealth (McPherson, 1983:44).

Preliterate societies usually showed great respect for elders as long as they proved useful to the group. Authority was given to the elderly because they could transmit their knowledge to the younger generation. But in a society living on the brink of subsistence, old people who outlived their usefulness became a burden. As societies developed in complexity, life expectancies increased and the elderly could be protected with power and property (Fischer, 1977:13). Where respect for age was not willingly given, it was entrenched in law or custom. With industrialization, societies experienced occupational changes, technological developments, and the growth of formalized retirement programs and benefits. In post-industrial society, however, the elderly regain some of the status and power that was previously threatened.

Preindustrial North Americans tended to place a relatively high value on youth, physical prowess, and independence from family (Fischer, 1977). Emigration from Great Britain or Europe often entailed a young man or young couple leaving elderly parents behind. Westward migration in North America involved breaking community ties, escaping traditional class barriers and behavioural codes, and moving away from the influence of older parents. However, since life expectancies were much lower in nineteenth century North America, many parents died before their children left home or married, and even when older parents were still alive, they often lived far away from their grown children. Older parents were best able to maintain the respect of and control over their children if they held specialized knowledge or controlled property or family money.

Despite the lack of agreement on the relationship between modernization and aging, the role of the elderly has definitely varied in different cultures. Societies that have experienced high rates of immigration and job migration, such as Canada, the United States, and Australia, have tended to reward physical strength, flexibility, and youthfulness, even though certain ethnic groups within these countries have emphasized respect for elders. On the other hand, societies with low rates of geographic and job mobility have often focused on traditional and religious values, and the elderly have been held in reverence. For example, in Japan, despite industrialization, respect for the elderly and the three-generation family is still important (Rhoads, 1984). Yet there are indications that the elderly parent living with her children often lacks privacy, is economically dependent on her children, and frequently experiences conflict with her daughter-in-law. Moreover, increasing rates of suicide among the elderly may be one indication of their psychological distress and declining status in Japan (Plath, 1972).

The early versions of modernization theory, which stated that the status of the elderly generally falls with modernization, have certainly generated considerable research in anthropology and social policy. Some researchers have argued that the theory is too simplistic. For example, Neysmith and Edwardh (1983) criticize modernization theory because they say it implies that underdevelopment is the fault of the characteristics of individuals rather than the social and economic relations binding Third World countries to the industrial world. They argue that dependency theory, a version of the political economy approach, would provide a more appropriate explanation of how older people live in the Third World

(Marshall, 1987). Other researchers argue that the status of the elderly is not necessarily based on modernization, but rather related to the balance between the cost of supporting the elderly and the social contributions they are perceived as making (Amoss, 1981; Foner, 1984; Vanderburgh, 1987). The high status of elders may continue despite modernization if certain political movements are developed or policy decisions made. In some Indian tribes in Canada, for example, the status of elders has been maintained with a resurgence of political awareness of minority rights and government support for multiculturalism (Amoss, 1981; Vanderburgh, 1987).

In other words, a controversy still exists about how the status of the elderly changes as a society modernizes and industrializes. We feel that demographic factors such as the relative size of the elderly population are important to elevating their status, but that a society's economic prosperity, which enables governments to develop social-security benefits, is also significant. The conclusion that the balance between the cost of supporting the elderly and their perceived social contribution actually encompasses both of these concerns. In the next section we will look at the socio-economic status of the elderly in present day Canadian society.

THE SOCIO-ECONOMIC STATUS OF THE ELDERLY IN CANADA

Demographic Trends

Since the Second World War the percentage of elderly people in the population has been rising gradually in Canada. There is, however, considerable provincial variation. Prince Edward Island has the largest proportion of elderly people at over 12 percent, followed by Saskatchewan and Manitoba as Table 3.1 indicates. Many younger people have left these provinces in search of education and work, but falling birth rates, increased life expectancy, and internal migration are responsible for high dependency ratios for the elderly. With the rise in the proportion of elderly people in the population, many provincial governments have been forced to increase social-security benefits and provide special programs for the elderly, such as home-care programs, nursing homes, and geriatric centres.

Canadian women can now expect to live about seven years longer than men if we look at life expectancies at birth. Although part of this discrepancy could relate to physiological differences, we know that males engage in more dangerous recreational and occupational activities. More males than females smoke cigarettes, drink alcohol to excess, work in dangerous manual labour jobs, work overtime, and engage in a whole series of dangerous sports activities. Males tend to postpone visiting their doctor until they have a serious disease. They are also less likely than

TABLE 3.1

Population 65 and Over by Province and Territory, Canada, 1981

	Number	As Percentage of Population
Newfoundland	43 780	7.7%
Prince Edward Island	14 895	12.2
Nova Scotia	92 555	10.9
New Brunswick	70 555	10.1
Québec	569 380	8.8
Ontario	868 190	10.1
Manitoba	121 820	11.9
Saskatchewan	116 170	12.0
Alberta	163 395	7.3
British Columbia	298 175	10.9
Yukon	735	3.2
Northwest Territories	1 320	2.9
CANADA	2 360 975	9.7

Source: National Council of Welfare. *Sixty-Five and Older.* Ottawa: February 1984, p. 18.

females to talk out emotional problems, which may exacerbate stress-related diseases. Some researchers suggest, however, that the gap is closing between the life expectancies of males and females with healthier lifestyles and medical breakthroughs.

The imbalance in the sex ratio among the elderly has important policy consequences. Over half of Canada's women aged seventy and over are widows compared to only one quarter of men in this age group. Women living alone constitute a major segment of households headed by older people, and this has increased substantially since the early 1960s. Whether this living situation is by choice or necessity, it requires a new attitude towards independence and aging. Older women may have to develop new skills such as automobile and home repairs, and a more assertive approach to financial investments or paid work. But governments are most concerned about the growing number of older women because they so often require public assistance.

Education and Employment

Throughout this century, each generation has been able to raise its educational attainment so that many older people have little formal schooling by today's standards. In 1981 over three quarters of those aged sixty-five and over had no degree, certificate, or diploma compared to about

FIGURE 3.1

**Percentage Distribution by Highest Level
of Schooling of the Elderly and Other Adult (25–64 Years)
Populations, Canada, 1981**

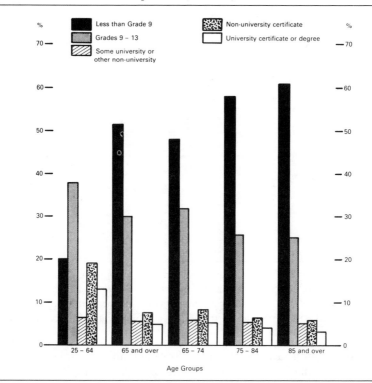

Source: Statistics Canada. *The Elderly in Canada*. Cat. 99–932. Ottawa: April
1984.

36 percent of those twenty-five to forty-four years old (Statistics Canada,
April 1984). The value in the labour market of graduating from school
has dramatically risen over the past two decades. Advanced education
has enabled young people to enter the labour force at a higher rank and
to be promoted faster, much to the chagrin of older, more experienced
but less educated workers.

Since the mid-1960s the labour force participation rates of men aged
fifty-five and over have gradually declined as mandatory retirement was
enforced and public and employer-sponsored pension plans were created
and expanded. The trend towards earlier retirement places a larger burden
on pension plans but creates more leisure time for elderly people. Women
aged fifty-five to sixty-four on the other hand, have gradually increased

TABLE 3.2

Labour Force Participation Rates, by Sex for
Selected Age Groups, Canada, 1966 to 1986*

	Males				
	1966	1971	1976	1981	1986
All Ages	79.9%	77.8%	77.6%	78.3%	76.7%
55 – 64	86.1	83.3	76.7	75.1	68.5
65 – 69	46.5	32.6	25.4	21.9	18.4
70+	14.6	12.1	9.8	8.9	7.6
	Females				
	1966	1971	1976	1981	1986
All Ages	33.6%	37.1%	45.2%	51.6%	55.1%
55 – 64	28.5	30.9	32.0	33.7	33.4
65 – 69	10.9	9.7	7.8	7.9	7.1
70+	3.2	2.6	2.2	2.5	1.9

* Annual Averages

Source: Health and Welfare Canada. *Fact Book on Aging in Canada*. Ottawa:
1983, p. 37. Statistics Canada. *The Labour Force*. December 1986,
Cat. 71–001. Ottawa: Supply and Services, January 1987, p. 84. Reproduced with permission of the Minister of Supply and Services Canada.

their participation rates in the labour force as Table 3.2 indicates. Discrimination in the workplace has lessened for older married women and
the rising cost of living has necessitated two incomes in many families.
Increased labour force participation will provide women with greater
financial security in their old age but will make them unavailable for
volunteer work such as caring for their elderly parents or spouse.

In general, about 2 percent of workers in all occupational categories
in the Canadian labour force were over the age of sixty-five in 1981. An
analysis of those occupations that have an over-representation of workers
who are sixty-five and over indicates that certain characteristics of these
occupations enable the elderly to continue working. For example, where
there is an emphasis on seniority, experience, and knowledge such as in
managerial and administrative positions, older workers are over-repre-
sented. Among the self-employed, such as doctors, lawyers, artists, and
musicians, there are high proportions of older workers. Where there is
a higher statutory retirement age, such as among federally-appointed
judges or senators, there are higher than average proportions of older
workers and the same is true for jobs with flexible work-scheduling. In

occupations with a low incidence of pension coverage and low career earnings, early retirement is less likely to occur because employees cannot afford to stop working. Staying in the labour force after the age of sixty-five depends largely on the structural characteristics of the occupation, such as the official retirement age or an emphasis on seniority, rather than simply on personal attitudes (Chen, 1985).

The treatment of elderly workers varies considerably with the relationship between the occupation and the economy. While emerging technologies tend to prefer hiring young workers rather than retraining older ones (Chen, 1987), some industrial sectors dependent on skilled labour need older workers with experience and highly developed skills and prefer to share work rather than promote early retirement (Stryckman, 1987). In semi-professions such as teaching, unions protect older employees from redundancy with seniority rules, which has led to intergenerational conflict within the occupation. But until recently, the popularity of early retirement in teaching has been curtailed by financial penalties, although these will undoubtedly be reduced or eliminated in the near future (Tindale, 1987). Older workers employed in secondary labour market jobs, typified by labour intensive, non-unionized, and low paid work, are more vulnerable to lay-off or retirement with negligible or no pension benefits.

While unemployment rates are generally lower for those aged fifty-five and over, the duration of unemployment is longer if they lose their job (Health and Welfare, 1983). Ageism sometimes prevents the unemployed worker over the age of forty from finding work; and the older the worker, the more difficulty in finding employment. Although older workers may not adapt as readily to new technology, they are generally more stable, reliable, consistent, and loyal employees than younger workers (Hendricks and Hendricks, 1977; Koyl, 1977).

Opportunities to work part-time have increased for both sexes, but especially for women. One problem with women taking part-time work after re-entering the labour force, however, is that benefits such as pension plan membership are not always available. But re-entrance into the labour force has enabled many older women to improve their standard of living and perhaps to put away some savings for retirement. Gradual retirement programs involving part-time work and partial pension benefits are being initiated by some employers, but since pension benefits are often based on the highest few years of earnings, employees are understandably reluctant to jeopardize their incomes in their preretirement years.

Some private companies and departments of the government have encouraged early retirement essentially to provide jobs for younger people and to save money. But these programs are usually offered only to higher status employees. Ironically, those in lower status and lower paid positions would probably be more likely to take advantage of such programs, since they usually report reduced levels of work satisfaction. Perhaps

TABLE 3.3

Average Income by Age and Sex
1985, Canada

Age	All individuals	Males	Females
24 & under	$ 8 446	$ 9 442	$ 7 373
25 – 34	19 585	23 973	14 603
35 – 44	24 130	30 933	16 183
45 – 54	23 476	30 777	14 369
55 – 59	21 213	27 373	13 200
60 – 64	17 330	23 749	10 421
65 & over	12 809	16 114	10 301
65 – 69	14 002	18 765	9 954
70 & over	12 154	14 508	10 477

Source: Statistics Canada. *Income Distribution by Size in Canada*, (Preliminary Estimates, 1985). Cat. 13–206. Ottawa: September 1986, p. 26.

employers fear that too many workers in some occupations would take advantage of early retirement programs if they were introduced at all levels.

The Elderly as Earners and Consumers

Income in Canada tends to fluctuate considerably by age and sex as Table 3.3 indicates. In 1985 those thirty-five to forty-four years of age had the highest incomes, perhaps indicating this generation's higher educational levels. For men, the main drop in income comes after age sixty-five, but for women it comes after age sixty, since women generally retire earlier than men. Looking at this static picture of the relationship between income and age should not allow us to forget that many individual workers' incomes rise with age. Those with occupations involving career mobility generally receive promotional and cost of living increases as they get older. Those with investment earnings often increase their income as interest rates rise or compound interest accumulates. Compared to earlier generations of elderly people, the elderly today have a higher standard of living. But despite improvements in pensions and other social-security benefits over the last few decades, retirement still means a substantial decline in income for most people. Since pension coverage is being expanded, however, retirement may not be as financially consequential in the future.

Table 3.4 shows the sources of income for elderly couples and unattached individuals in 1981. Unattached women were least likely to be living on their earnings or employer pensions, since they were least likely to be employed in their younger years. Over one half of their income came from government pensions, which is a central concern to policymakers.

TABLE 3.4

Percentage Distribution of Money Income by Source,
for Married Couples and Unattached Individuals
Aged 66 and Over, by Sex, Canada, 1981

Source of Income	Married Couples	Unattached Men	Unattached Women
Earnings	15%	9%	5%
Investments	28	28	31
Old Age Security/ Guaranteed Income Supplement	30	32	43
Canada Pension Plan	10	11	7
Pensions from Employers and Annuities	13	16	9
Other Government Transfers	2	3	3
All Other	1	1	2
Average Income	$17 900	$10 900	$8 800

Source: Health and Welfare Canada. *Fact Book on Aging in Canada*. Ottawa: 1983, p. 47. Reproduced with permission of the Minister of Supply and Services Canada.

Despite lower incomes than younger people, the incomes of elderly people have risen considerably in the past few decades. Indexed public pensions, improved private pensions, and high interest rates have given some retired people more income than when they were working. The elderly population also has a higher than average rate of home ownership. Their homes, however, are likely to be older; to need repair; and to contain fewer facilities such as microwave ovens, dishwashers, automatic washers, and record players. Elderly people are also less likely to own automobiles. Not owning a car can keep elderly people housebound where public transit does not exist or is inconveniently scheduled.

Until recently the needs of older people in the market-place have received limited attention (Lumpkin, 1984). In previous research the elderly have been characterized as economy conscious, but this may be particularly true for those on fixed incomes rather than the substantial portion with high incomes. Some studies have suggested that the elderly desire special treatment when shopping, especially convenient store location, rest facilities, smaller-sized packages of perishables, larger print for labels, drugs without child-proof caps, and parcel carry-out (Gelb, 1978; Mason and Bearden, 1978). Other researchers have noted that older people are less likely to use credit cards than younger shoppers (Bernhardt and Kinnear, 1977). The elderly appear to enjoy shopping less than younger age groups and do not use shopping as a form of recreation as adolescents frequently do. But inconsistencies in the research on the elderly as consumers reinforces the idea that the elderly are not a homogeneous group (Towle and Martin, 1975).

Television has become a good companion for many older people. Because the elderly are heavy consumers of the media (McPherson and Kozlik, 1987), depictions of old age and the elderly may have negative consequences for the elderly's self-image, such as contributing to self-doubt and feelings of powerlessness. Research has well-documented both the low frequency with which older people appear on North American television and the relatively negative ways in which they are most frequently portrayed (Gerbner et al., 1980; Atchley, 1983; Elliott, 1984; Holtzman and Akiyama, 1985; Powell and Williamson, 1985). Public policies that dictate whether distorted images are permissable in prime-time programming may be important in affecting whether the status of the elderly will be improved or down-graded (Powell and Williamson, 1985).

Health Status, Lifestyle, and Attitudes

In the last century Canadians have experienced rapid declines in mortality, especially in infant and maternal mortality and fatal diseases in childhood and middle age. Whether these declines will continue is debatable, but biomedical breakthroughs in the prevention and treatment of senile dementia and osteoporosis could radically change the quality of life and need for institutional care for some elderly people (Health and Welfare Canada, 1982:45). By using measures of health care and illness such as "bed-days" in hospitals, "disability days," or "activity-loss days," those over sixty-five are definitely less healthy than younger people. The elderly have higher rates of hospital utilization, longer stays in hospitals, and also make more frequent visits to medical doctors than younger people; but researchers remind us that only a fraction of very old people are using a disproportionate amount of health resources. Furthermore, hospital costs account for about half of the health-care expenses in Canada (Chappell, 1987). Health-care officials have been particularly concerned about the rising cost of health facilities for a growing older population, but a controversy still exists about whether or not a higher proportion of elderly people will actually need chronic care or medical attention in the future.

Despite the fact that more older than younger people suffer from chronic ailments, the majority of elderly people function well until advanced age and do not rely on formal support services (Connidis, 1985). Many of those who consider themselves in good health, however, still suffer from chronic diseases such as arthritis or rheumatism. From surveys of nursing home patients, it seems that some patients simply lack alternative care and could function in group homes or in their own homes without intensive medical services. After all, health needs are not the sole determinants of nursing home use. Social characteristics such as the availability of a spouse and ability to cope alone are also important (Shapiro and Roos, 1987), as well as the income level of the family. But the social and health services available to older people who choose to stay in their own homes are insufficient. Senior citizen apartments with nursing and homemaker services often have long waiting lists and many older people are unaware of provincial government home-care programs.

As people age, their lifestyle becomes more sedentary and home-centred (McPherson and Kozlik, 1987). Canadians aged sixty-five and over are less likely than younger age groups to go out to dinner or to the theatre, less likely to move their residence (as Table 3.5 indicates), and less likely to engage in physical sports or exercise. There is some evidence, however, *Activities* that older people specialize in particular sports and physical activities and spend more time on fewer activities as they age (Curtis and White, 1984). But older Canadians spend the majority of their leisure time visiting or talking with friends and relatives (Health and Welfare Canada, 1983:86), and those who live alone are just as likely to be socially active as those who live together (Delisle, 1982). The leisure activities of the

TABLE 3.5

"Mobility Rates"* per 1000 Population
of a Given Age Group
Selected Population Movements, Canada, 1981

	Rates Per 1000 Population	
	5 – 64 Years Old	65 + Years Old
All movers within Canada	473.2	247.9
Urban to rural	47.8	17.9
Rural to urban	35.2	20.8
Urban to urban	341.2	187.4
Rural to rural	49.0	21.7
All interprovincial migrants	54.8	18.0
All provinces to B.C.	11.0	5.8
All provinces to Ont.	11.9	5.5
Quebec to Ontario	5.7	4.0

* "Mobility Rates" are computed as the number of persons who reported a 1981 address different from their 1976 address per 1000 population.

Source: Statistics Canada. *The Elderly in Canada*. Cat. 99–932. Ottawa: April 1984.

elderly, however, depend to a great extent on their previous lifestyle, interests, and activities. Those with more education tend to be more active. They are especially likely to engage in reading, studying, exercising, entertaining, and driving more often than the less-educated elderly. But leisure activities among the elderly also depend on their health, their former occupation, their ethnicity, their marital status, and their access to transportation (Roadburg, 1985).

Reduced physical activity with increasing age has social and cultural as well as physiological bases. Attitudes about suitable adult activity, time constraints, lack of facilities and partners for adult sports, and fears concerning the safety and suitability of exercise (Myers and Gonda, 1986) discourage many adults and elderly people from remaining active. Although lack of exercise is related to poorer mental and physical health, most older people are not noticeably unhealthy. Tables 3.6 and 3.7 present figures from two Canadian government studies showing that participation in sports and exercise tends to decline with age, but the relationship is not a clear one. The results of the 1981 survey indicate that activity levels do not vary substantially after the age of thirty, although the 1976

TABLE 3.6

Percent of Canadian Population Participating in Sport and Physical Recreation or Exercise Activities by Age, October 1976

Age	Sport and Physical Recreation Activities[1]	Exercise Activities[2]
14 years	84.2%	89.3%
15 – 16	82.0	86.9
17 – 19	73.3	75.4
20 – 24	66.3	63.4
25 – 34	61.3	62.3
35 – 44	51.2	53.3
45 – 54	37.2	50.1
55 – 64	24.5	45.7
65 and over	9.7	37.0
Total Population	42.7%	58.7%

1. Participation in one or more sport or physical recreation activities at least once during the 12 months preceding the survey.
2. Participation in one or more exercise activities at least once during the month preceding the survey.

Source: Statistics Canada. *Culture Statistics, Recreational Activities, 1976.* Cat. 87–501. Ottawa: November 1978, p. 10. Reproduced with permission of the Minister of Supply and Services Canada.

TABLE 3.7

Leisure-Time Physical Activity in Canada,
Age 20+, 1981

Age & Sex		Sedentary	Minimally Active	Adequately Active
20 – 29	M	50.4%	18.1%	31.5%
	F	61.1	20.2	21.4
30 – 39	M	62.3	14.3	23.4
	F	69.2	17.5	14.6
40 – 49	M	66.9	15.9	17.2
	F	69.1	16.2	14.6
50 – 59	M	66.0	16.6	17.4
	F	68.1	16.2	16.1
60 +	M	59.0	17.7	23.4
	F	68.8	15.8	15.8

Source: T. Stephens, C.L. Craig, B.F. Ferris. "Adult Physical Activity in Canada: Findings from the Canada Fitness Survey I" *Canadian Journal of Public Health* 77, July/August 1986, p. 287.

study showed more of a decline with age. Unfortunately the measures of activity and exercise were not comparable in these two studies. But there is other evidence that more older people are remaining active and are exercising regularly than a few decades ago.

Although older people are far less likely than younger people to be the victims of personal crimes such as theft or assault as Table 3.8 indicates, they fear victimization more than younger people. Media coverage

TABLE 3.8

Victimization Rates per 1000 Population
for Selected Types of Personal Crimes for
Selected Age Groups, Canada, 1981

Personal Crimes	Age Groups	
	Less Than 65	65 and Over
Theft of Personal Property	71	13
Assault	58	8
Robbery	10	4
Sexual Assault	4	—

Source: Health and Welfare Canada. *Fact Book on Aging in Canada.* Ottawa: 1983, p. 83. Reproduced with permission of the Minister of Supply and Services Canada.

of serious crimes and swindles against the elderly promote this fear of victimization, but the lower rates of personal victimization among the elderly generally relate to lifestyle. By this we mean that older people seldom walk in the street at night, avoid high crime environments, and generally spend more time at home. Elderly men who live in the street are most at risk, but most older people spend less time in the streets than younger age groups. However, lessened physical strength and mobility make older people less able to defend themselves and therefore more fearful of violence.

Attitudes towards established religions and church attendance also vary considerably by age. Bibby (1983) found that from 1946 to 1981, the percentage of Canadians who attended church weekly declined from 67 percent to 27 percent and while only 15 percent of Canadian adults under the age of thirty were weekly attenders, 45 percent of those aged sixty and over attended weekly. To some elderly people, church services provide a major social outing and may help them cope with grief and death. Bibby also found that while two thirds of adults said they attended religious services regularly as children, only one third of those with school-age children were exposing them to religious instruction. This suggests that a declining proportion of Canadians are being exposed to a religious view of the world, since no other social institution has taken over religious socialization. What impact this will have on young people as they age is difficult to say. One could speculate that different belief systems such as faith in science or astrology, or a humanistic philosophy may become more important to the future elderly, since increasing numbers of younger people are turning away from established religions.

There is a controversy in the literature on the relationship between religious beliefs and aging. Most studies have found that attendance at religious ceremonies remains stable over the lifetime or declines somewhat in later years because of poor health or transportation problems. Yet

TABLE 3.9

Church Attendance by Age (in %)					
Age	Total Number	Weekly	Monthly	Yearly	Never
18 – 29	225	15	7	55	23
30 – 39	345	18	8	50	24
40 – 49	172	26	8	46	20
50 – 59	172	36	14	37	13
60 +	278	45	9	35	11
Totals	1192	27	9	45	19

Source: Reginald W. Bibby. "Religionless Christianity: A Profile of Religion in the Canadian 80s", *Social Indicators Research* 13 (July) 1983:1–16.

older people report strong religious beliefs, which could reflect either a cohort difference or a psychological consequence of aging. As people approach death, they may feel a greater need for belief in God and an afterlife to compensate for the loss of friends and relatives, but alternatively, they could have been raised in an era of stronger institutionalized religions and the expectation of church attendance. Other studies indicate that certain groups of people seem to attend religious services more frequently at all ages, such as women, Catholics, the less-educated, and those who live in rural areas (McPherson, 1983:423–424).

The lifestyles of elderly people are influenced by social, psychological, environmental, and physiological factors, especially one's health, financial situation, occupation, attitudes, relationships, and cultural background. But measuring the health of elderly people is also influenced by services within the present health-care system. Official statistics of "bed-days" or use of health-care resources do not explain why certain groups of people use more health resources, just that they do. Hospitalization for chronic-care patients could be a result of a lack of home-care facilities. The decision to use advanced technology to prolong the lives of dying patients is a social and political judgement made by doctors, hospital administrators, and provincial governments for a variety of reasons, but it increases "bed-days" for elderly people. It may be possible to alter both lifestyles and the health-care system so that old age would not need to be "medicalized" to the same extent. Improved preventative health care, increased community services, and higher educational levels may radically change older people's lifestyles in the future and our subsequent stereotypes about aging.

Ethnic Variations

When discussing the status of the elderly, it is important to keep in mind the many cultural and ethnic groups that make up Canada's population. The way in which these different groups deal with aging and the elderly varies with their cultural tradition, their socio-economic position, and the proportion of elderly people in their populations. The proportion of elderly people is particularly high among certain ethnic groups such as the Jewish, 16 percent; the Polish, 15 percent; and the Ukrainian, 14 percent (Statistics Canada, April 1984). This reflects the periods of heavy immigration in the earlier part of this century, and in the case of Jewish people, their low fertility rates. Immigrants who came to Canada after World War II — such as Italians and Chinese, with 7 percent aged sixty-five and over — generally have lower proportions of elderly people and less-developed social clubs and retirement homes for them. As the proportion of elderly immigrants rises, their ethnic groups will probably develop more facilities for them, but in the meantime, care of the elderly usually falls on the extended family.

One major ethnic difference in the lifestyles of the elderly relates to institutionalization versus living in a three-generation family. Groups with low fertility rates, high incomes, and a high percentage of elderly people often have a well-developed system of senior citizen facilities. This has particularly been true for Jewish people in Canada. On the other hand, groups that have higher fertility rates, large extended families, lower incomes, and lower proportions of elderly people — such as Italians, Greeks, Chinese, French Canadians, and native North Americans — have preferred the three-generation family to institutional life for the elderly. Older parents, especially grandmothers, often live with their adult children after widowhood and perform domestic tasks such as babysitting and household maintenance. Living alone in old age is seen as undesirable in groups with extended families, even when the alternative is to be financially dependent and to lack privacy in their children's home.

Attitudes to death also vary by ethnicity and cultural group. In Inuit society prior to European contact, the elderly lost their importance when they were no longer able to contribute to food production, culture, or personal services. In a subsistence-level society, it was important that the elderly not take food away from children or the group could not continue. Therefore, the elderly were allowed to wander off or to gradually reduce their food intake to the point of death if the group was suffering from a food shortage or the older person was terminally ill. In recent years, with a more sedentary lifestyle, improved food distribution, and more accessible health services, life expectancies among the Inuit have increased. Yet the lifespan for native people remains lower than for most Canadians. Lower native life expectancies are related to poor nutrition, unsanitary living conditions, dangerous manual labour occupations, and high rates of violence and poverty. At the same time, birth rates are much higher than the national average, and the native population is not aging but growing younger on average (Frideres, 1983). This means that government policies and programs for the country as a whole must not jeopardize the opposite demographic trends of native people. Considering the Canadian government's track record in the past, this will be quite a challenge.

Canadian ethnic groups also differ in their respect for the elderly (Driedger and Chappell, 1987). Those from Oriental cultures, for example, have continued their tradition of respect even when the older person is financially dependent on adult children. Other cultural groups, such as Italians, Hutterites, Greeks, and Portuguese, place a strong emphasis on the authority of the eldest male. But the generation and culture gap between immigrants and their Canadian-born children often becomes a source of contention among family members, especially over issues such as this. The generation born and educated in Canada has greater opportunities for intermarriage and occupational mobility and will undoubtedly change some of these traditions. The second generation consequently faces a different situation when they grow old.

Because of job discrimination, low education, and language problems, many older ethnic group members occupied low status positions in the labour force and consequently retired with no work pensions. However, some first generation immigrants were able to save money for their retirement through a life of frugality, mutual assistance, or entrepreneurial activity, or at least provide greater economic security for their children. The economic status of the ethnic elderly depends very much on the group's educational levels and the jobs they first occupied in Canada. For example, while older British and Jewish immigrants are among the wealthiest, some cultural groups such as native people and southern Europeans have remained relatively poor regardless of age. The reasons why some groups have not moved up the economic status ladder have been related to institutional constraints such as educational channelling, hiring through "old boy ties," and racism (Driedger and Mezoff, 1981; Driedger and Chappell, 1987).

Despite the fact that we have talked about the status of the elderly in Canada, we must emphasize that ethnic and cultural variations make generalizations difficult. Even within ethnic groups, differences based on gender, generation, place of residence, and socio-economic status obscure the general conclusions about how the status of the elderly varies by cultural group. Future studies of ethnic variations will have to consider that recent immigrants to Canada have come from different countries than today's elderly immigrants and have experienced different power relations with the dominant group (Ujimoto, 1987).

The Elderly and Political Power

As the proportion of elderly people rises in industrialized countries, more opportunities are available for a "grey power" movement to develop. Older voters in Canada have been more partisan than younger ones and have been less likely to change their vote over successive elections (Johnston, 1986). These trends can probably be attributed to the cumulative reinforcement of early political experiences and selective perception later in life. Social, occupational, and geographic mobility are generally greatest in young adulthood, and mobility may help to develop political attitudes. Because of their diverse backgrounds and interests, however, the elderly seldom vote as a block (James, 1985).

In areas of specific concern such as pensions, the voice of the elderly is collectively strong and has clearly reached the ears of the politicians. For example, in 1985 United Senior Citizens of Ontario released a five-year study of the life conditions and concerns of elderly people in that province. The major concern they found was the inadequacy of retirement incomes. Of those surveyed, 42 percent were living below the poverty line set by the National Council of Welfare. The second major concern was the limited access by elderly people to home-support and home-care services. While the majority of respondents owned their own homes,

t they would have to go into institutions because they
ɟ the high cost of home care (Anderson, 1985). These
)f concern to elderly people in other provinces and coun-
ɩcians and social service workers are searching for polit-
ɩle and affordable solutions.

increasing political awareness and organization among the
ᴄɪₑ   ɩe more evident when the Mulroney government tried to
partially deindex Old Age Security in 1985. The virtually unanimous
condemnation of deindexation by all age groups indicated that intergenerational conflict is unlikely to occur over the pension issue (Gifford,
1985). Since over half of Canadian voters are over forty years old, and
considering the popularity of early retirement and the value placed on
independence for the elderly in this country, "pension consciousness" is
relatively high. But pensioners are beginning to unite over other issues
as well, such as the changes to the federal drug patent act, which many
groups feel will substantially raise the price of prescription drugs (Pratt,
1987). The increasing political importance of the elderly is also apparent
in the recent appointment of George Hees to the Ministry of State for
Senior Citizens in August 1987.

In recent years a number of new senior citizen and pensioner organizations have mushroomed across the country to add strength to the voice
of existing groups. These organizations, such as United Senior Citizens
of Ontario, Association Québécoise pour la défense des droits des retraités
et préretraités, The Canadian Council of Retirees, Canadian Pensioners
Concerned, The National Federation of Pensioners and Senior Citizens,
and Fédération de l'age d'or du Québec, have recently received media
attention over the deindexation issue, which has raised their political
profile. Pensioners, however, have been organized for years. The National
Federation of Pensioners and Senior Citizens has existed since 1945. In
the United States the National Council on Aging was established in the
1930s as a lobby group for the elderly. American pensioners' organizations have generally been more involved in research and lobbying than
Canadian groups, perhaps because they are larger and have acquired
more resources. The American Association of Retired Persons, for example, has attracted seventeen million members and the National Council
of Senior Citizens has four million.

In the United States the nascent social movement to combat ageism
has been heavily influenced by feminist models for social change and
well-populated by feminist activists (Reinharz, 1986). Advocates of the
elderly such as Maggie Kuhn, national convenor of the Gray Panthers,
have been concerned with nursing home reform, the development of
national health insurance, improved housing, environmental protection,
and nuclear disarmament. Kuhn questions the value of special social
services for the elderly, which she calls "novocaine," and prefers the

formation of age-integrated political action groups (Kuhn, 1984; Reinharz, 1986).

In Canada a strong nationwide organization has been inhibited by language barriers, geographic distance, and the lack of strong leadership. Anglophone organizations have depended on volunteer leaders who are not as attuned to the government decision-making process as the more professional activists usually are. On the other hand, the Fédération de l'age d'or du Québec differs from other Canadian organizations with its professional leadership and more aggressive tactics (Gifford, 1985).

Both federal and provincial governments in Canada have appointed advisory councils on aging. Although since 1984 the National Advisory Council of Aging has become more politically active than the government had expected (Verzuh, 1985), these councils and pensioners groups have less impact on the legislative process than similar groups in other countries. In Britain, for example, the national lobby group called Age Concern has been as influential in policy issues as the Gray Panthers in the United States (Gifford, 1985).

Where political parties or unions have supported and sponsored the pensioners' movement such as they have in Britain, Austria, Sweden, and France, the elderly are likely to have greater political power. Similarly, where organizations such as the Gray Panthers in the United States are able to collect substantial membership fees, they can more easily fund research and lobbying efforts. While the Canadian movement lacks this sponsorship and resource base, their political consciousness is growing.

CONCLUSION

The socio-economic status of the elderly has varied by cultural group and historical era. While some researchers have argued that the most important variable influencing the changing status of the elderly has been modernization, others have suggested that this theory is far too simplistic. The status of the elderly is not necessarily related only to modernization but also to the size of the elderly population, their level of political and social awareness, and the policy decisions affecting their lives. The balance between the cost of supporting the elderly and the social contribution they are perceived as making seems to be a more realistic explanation of their status. Using social exchange theory, therefore, may provide a more fruitful explanation of their status than relying on a structural theory such as the modernization thesis.

The present generation of elderly people in Canada has lived through a major economic depression and the Second World War. These economic and political events undoubtedly shaped their attitudes and values, affected their educational attainment, and perhaps even their marriage plans.

Generally, today's elderly people are less educated and have lower incomes than those under sixty-five years of age. Because they grew up without social-security programs that are now taken for granted, many of today's elderly people are cautious about saving money, frugal in their spending, and often more censorious of the lifestyles of younger generations.

Since the Second World War the population has been noticeably aging and older workers must now compete with those younger and more educated. In order to reduce the older workforce, employers needed the assistance of governments and younger employees. The development of contributory and old-age pensions assisted employers to retire older workers and enabled the elderly to live without paid work. But as the percentage of elderly people in the population grows, their demands for improved pensions and health care are more difficult for governments to ignore. Both the elderly and organizations catering to their needs are now fighting for scarce public resources with those representing the needs of younger people.

In a country such as Canada with a growing proportion of elderly residents, policy-makers need to understand the life patterns of the elderly and need to be concerned about the availability and cost of social and health services for this age group. Governments now provide income supplements for the elderly and subsidize their cost of living to a great extent, but with an increasing proportion of elderly people in the population, an estimate of future services must be planned well ahead of time.

In the next chapter we will discuss social legislation and public policy related to retirement and pension benefits, medical and health services, and housing and community services. We will also compare Canada's programs for the elderly to those in other countries.

4

AGING AND SOCIAL POLICY

INTRODUCTION

The problems of old age have primarily been seen by governments as poverty and the decline in health. In countries such as the United States and Canada, the nineteenth century solution to this problem was thought to be thrift throughout the entire life span. Yet saving sufficient money for old age has seldom been possible for most of the population (Myles and Boyd, 1982). Unemployment or unexpected illness often prevented families from paying their immediate bills and sometimes put them heavily into debt. Low wages and the absence of social-security benefits such as health, disability, or unemployment insurance meant that money saved for the future often had to be spent on necessities.

The social acceptance of old-age insurance, annuities, and health insurance in North America was delayed by the moral connotations placed on those unable to save for the future and by the political associations between government social insurance and socialism (Bryden, 1974:24). In this chapter we will take a historical look at the development of retirement, pension, and health insurance plans and their impact on elderly people.

RETIREMENT AND PENSION PLANS

Historical Background

Until the twentieth century, retirement from work before disability was generally a privilege for the rich. In the nineteenth century pensions were usually seen as favours for special categories of workers, such as military personnel who were given pensions for service to their country. But most private companies had no official retirement policies nor pension plans.

Long before the introduction of old-age pensions in North America, some European governments had initiated compulsory old-age insurance programs. For example, Germany introduced such a system in 1889, Austria in 1906, and Sweden in 1913. France had a national system of old-age support as early as 1850, and in Great Britain the question of old-age benefits became a political issue in the 1870s and continued to be one until they were implemented in 1908 (Fischer, 1977:161). In most cases, however, benefits were minimal and only supplemented the wages of older workers rather than replacing them (Myles, 1984:16).

Towards the end of the nineteenth century and early in the twentieth century, life expectancies increased, creating a larger percentage of older people in the population. At the same time, industrial growth was accompanied by a new emphasis on efficiency, fitness, and speed, which disadvantaged older workers (Achenbaum, 1978; Graebner, 1980). With the rise of scientific management, the labour process was deskilled, undermining the work organization of traditional craft production (Myles, 1984:12). Younger workers who could more readily adapt to the new technology were often preferred for the increasing number of factory jobs. Not surprisingly, the idea of universal retirement arose largely from the initiatives of social reformers, large industrialists, and social and economic analysts, rather than from the workers themselves (Haber, 1978:78). In some cases, the unions and workers actually opposed retirement because they could not survive on their meagre savings or the benefits provided by the state for the elderly.

The first large American company to establish a comprehensive retirement system was American Express in 1875, but other companies were slow to follow this precedent (Fischer, 1977:165). In 1908 old-age annuity plans were first available in Canada and by 1910 in the United States, yet very few people took advantage of them. High premiums and a low rate of return were largely to blame, but there was also a prevalent attitude that saving for old age should be possible without institutional support. Most North Americans prior to the Second World War worked until disability or death, or depended on their children for assistance. Having children was comparable to old-age insurance.

The demand for universal retirement and government assistance was given added impetus by the widespread unemployment of the 1930s Depression. Because many people lost their life-savings, confidence in the tradition of self-reliance and individual thrift was undermined (Ascah, 1984). Politicians realized that the causes of unemployment and declining income were not personal but were affected by national and international economic trends (Chappell, 1980). But it was post-World War II prosperity that allowed many countries to develop a system of income transfers to the elderly (Myles, 1984:13,17). With this development came a change in orientation from providing "assistance" to the elderly poor to the concept of "social security." Not surprisingly, rising rates of retirement corresponded with higher rates of government retirement benefits. In other words, most people could afford to retire when their post-retirement benefits more closely approximated their previous income.

The development of contributory pension plans allowed for increases in benefits as wages rose. In the late 1950s and 1960s old-age benefits were restructured, coverage was expanded, and benefits were increased in many industrialized countries (Guillemard, 1983).

Canadian Government Old–Age Benefits

During the 1920s, pension legislation was enacted in both the United States and Canada as more socially-minded ideas were introduced by European immigrants, life expectancies were increased, and more older workers were displaced by technological change. In 1927, despite lobbying by private insurance companies, the Canadian government shared the cost with the provinces for a "means-tested" pension (targeted at low-income people who did not own much property) for residents aged seventy and over. Since the average life expectancy was only about sixty years at that time, few people would have been eligible. It was not until 1952 that the government revised the Old Age Pension Act, providing a "flat-rate" pension to those aged seventy and over who met certain resident requirements. By a "flat-rate" pension, we mean that it was not graduated according to work history, income, or the financial need of the pensioner. After 1966, the age of eligibility was lowered to sixty-five for Old Age Security benefits.

The Canada and Quebec Pension Plans (CPP and QPP), which were introduced in 1966, are unlike the old-age pension in that they are related to lifetime earnings. Benefits are given principally to those who have worked in the labour force before reaching age sixty-five, although there is also a survivor benefit. Benefits for retired workers and their spouses are based on compulsory contributions by both employees and employers, and benefits vary by level of earnings. CPP/QPP benefits are calculated as being 25 percent of average lifetime earnings up to a maximum. The maximum income was intended to be the average industrial wage as measured by Statistics Canada, although the present limit is lower than that (Morton, 1984:6). In June 1986 changes were made to the CPP to create more flexibility in retirement age so that retirement at age sixty with partial benefits or retirement at age seventy with higher benefits would be possible. CPP pension credits earned during marriage can be shared at divorce or retirement at the request of one spouse, and survivor benefits will no longer be cut off at remarriage.

In the past decade the CPP and QPP have created huge funds that have become the principal source of debt-financing for provincial governments in Canada. This money is used to finance economic development; and managers of pension funds wield considerable economic power because of the amount of money involved. The expansion of the public pension system could potentially lead to the transfer of economic power from the business élite to the state, which explains some of the opposition

Most disapprove of de-indexing pensions, national survey shows

By *Sherri Barron*
Citizen *staff writer*

Just hours after Finance Minister Michael Wilson decided to back down Thursday on government plans to de-index pensions, a national poll confirmed that the government has made a wise move in the eyes of Canadians.

The first part of a national survey by Winnipeg-based Angus Reid Associates, commissioned by five Canadian newspapers including The Citizen *and released early this morning shows that 85 per cent of 1,892 Canadians polled disapproved of the government plan to de-index pensions for senior citizens.*

Only nine per cent of those surveyed, all 18 or over, said they approved the plan. Six per cent were unsure.

The opposition to de-indexing was universally high across the country, though respondents in Western Canada were slightly more likely than those in other regions to approve de-indexing.

But the drop in Mulroney's public appeal is particularly high among the elderly. Forty-seven per cent of those over 55 years of age said their opinion of him has grown worse since the election.

Thirty-six per cent of those between 35 and 54, and 32 per cent of those between 18 and 34 have lowered their opinion of him.

The survey also showed that only 30 per cent of the 48 per cent of people over 55 who voted Tory last fall would do so if an election were held now.

Asked whether they have come to trust Mulroney more or less, in terms of his commitment to take care of the poor, the elderly and those in economic trouble since he came into office, 72 per cent of the respondents said they trust him less.

His overall performance rating by region shows that negative opinion about him is highest in Atlantic Canada, Ontario and the West, and somewhat lower in Quebec.

When respondents were asked if their opinion of Mulroney has improved, remained the same or grown worse since the fall election, 48 per cent of the people surveyed said they feel the same way about him.

Thirty-seven per cent think less of him now. Only 13 per cent have a better impression of Mulroney.

Two per cent of the respondents were unsure.

Only 13 per cent said they now trust him more. The remainder of those polled were either unsure or said their perception of Mulroney hasn't changed.

Commissioned after Wilson announced the possible change in pension payments in his May 23 budget, the poll was conducted between June 20 and 25.

Angus Reid Associates is a national polling company in business since 1979. The company did polling for Opposition Leader John Turner during the last federal election.

There's a 95 per-cent-chance that results of such random surveys are within plus or minus three per centage points of what they would be if the entire Canadian population were polled.

The rest of the survey is to be released Saturday.

It includes a review of the political standings of the major political parties, what Canadians consider the good points about Mulroney and his government, and perceptions of both opposition parties and leaders.

Courtesy of *The Ottawa Citizen*, June 28, 1985.

---

from the business community to the expansion of public pensions (Myles and Boyd, 1982:278).

Despite the introduction of Old Age Security and CPP/QPP, numerous elderly Canadians were still living on low incomes. In 1967 the federal government tried to improve the incomes of the poorer elderly by introducing the Guaranteed Income Supplement (GIS), an income-tested pension equivalent to 40 percent of Old Age Security (OAS) for those aged sixty-five and over. However, there were still many couples in which the husband was receiving an old-age pension, but the wife was not yet old enough to qualify. The Spouse's Allowance (SPA) was initiated in 1975 to assist the spouses of pensioners who were between sixty and sixty-four years old and in financial need. Since that time, the SPA has been expanded to cover widows and widowers aged sixty to sixty-four, but not single or divorced elderly people in financial need, with the assumption that single and divorced people are more likely to have employer-sponsored pensions, savings, or to be in the work force.

Income tax exemptions for the elderly, initiated in 1948, have been raised over the years. OAS, GIS, and SPA have all increased with the Consumer Price Index since 1973. Although the government announced partial deindexation of the OAS in May 1985, the decision was later rescinded because of public outcry and an organized lobby by pensioners' associations. In Table 4.1 we can see the October 1987 value of monthly payments to the elderly in Canada. While everyone sixty-five years of age and over who meets certain residence requirements is eligible to

TABLE 4.1

Monthly Benefits for Elderly from Canadian Government Programs, October 1987

A.	Old Age Security	$308.19
	— universal program	
B.	Guaranteed Income Supplement	
	— income-tested	
	1) single person or married person whose spouse is not a recipient of OAS or SPA	366.28
	2) married person whose spouse is recipient of OAS	238.56
C.	Spouse's Allowance	
	— income-tested	
	1) maximum amount for spouses	546.75
	2) maximum for widows/widowers	603.63
D.	Canada Pension Plan	
	— earning's related	
	1) maximum retirement benefit at age 65	521.52
	2) maximum survivor's benefit	
	(65 and over)	312.91
	(under 65)	290.36
	3) maximum death benefit	2590.00

Note: Benefits A, B, and C are adjusted every three months based on recent changes in the Consumer Price Index, Benefit D is adjusted annually.

Source: Health and Welfare Canada, Claims and Benefits Division, Ottawa.

receive Old Age Security, the other benefits are based on low income or previous earnings.

As more people reach the age of sixty-five, concerns have been expressed about the actuarial base of public pensions and their ability to rise with the cost of living. Pension plans are based on the idea that each generation will be supported by the one that follows. This means that when the baby-boom generation retires in the 2020s and 2030s, their pensions will come from the pockets of the smaller "baby-bust" generation born in the 1970s and 1980s. It has been suggested that by the year 2021 the cost of public pensions could increase at least three and a half times (McDaniel, 1986:69). But in the meantime, the working age population is increasing slightly and decision-makers should have time to bolster pension funds for the increase expected after 2020.

In a 1986 study of seven major industrial countries for the International Monetary Fund, projections from 1980 to 2025 indicate a significant increase in the ratio of government social expenditures to the Gross

Domestic Product (GDP) in most countries except Canada. Sharp increases in these expenditures are predicted, especially for European countries and Japan, taking into account the aging population, the 1980 level of expenditures, and certain assumptions about productivity. In Canada social expenditures are expected to decrease relative to GDP until 2021 and then to increase moderately for the next fifteen years. The ratio of public pension expenditures to GDP is actually predicted to decline until 2010, because of the expanding working population, and then to rise by 40 percent from 2010 to 2025 (Heller et al., 1986:4–6, 31). Real pension expenditures are expected to have increased to over three times the 1980 level by 2025, but the GDP is also expected to have risen. In comparison with countries such as Japan and Italy, however, this anticipated increase in the cost of public pensions is relatively small.

The "crisis" in public pensions has definitely been aggrandized by the media. It could be averted by raising Canada Pension Plan contributions or taxes, by raising the retirement age, by assisting women to enter and stay in the labour force so that they would receive the Canada Pension Plan or an employer-sponsored pension, or by expanding the coverage and benefits of private pensions. As well, projections of the proportion of elderly people in the future can provide the basis for strategies for future social-security expenses. Because these strategies depend on political decisions, they will involve considerable consultation and negotiation and will not be based only on statistical trends.

The public protest against the proposal to partially deindex the old-age pension in 1985 implied that support for continuing facilities and services to the elderly was strong. After all, if pensions were cut back, not only the elderly would suffer. Younger people would have to assist financially their aging parents and worry about their own economic future. Brought up to take old-age pensions and other social-security benefits for granted, many young people have virtually no savings, even when they earn above average incomes, and few belong to employer-sponsored pension plans. After the federal government rescinded the earlier decision to partially deindex Old Age Security, premiums for the Canada Pension Plan were raised. Through this decision, the financial future of public pensions was reinforced and solidified.

The Canadian pension system is, however, one of the least generous among Western nations. In a study of seventeen industrialized member nations of OECD, Canada ranked fourteenth in the relative benefit levels provided through state social-insurance schemes. For widows, Canadian benefits were even worse in comparison to these other countries (OECD, 1976:22). Income security payments are too low to provide an adequate standard of living and have not eradicated the very distinctions between the rich and the poor that they were designed to eliminate (Chappell, 1987). Canada's relatively youthful population is one factor contributing to inadequate public pension plans, but another may be the heavy reliance on private savings.

Private Pensions and Retirement Savings

Some employers or unions have established pension plans in which the employer shares the cost of contributions with employees, but other pension plans are "non-contributory," which means that employers pay for the entire pension plan and employees lose their benefits if they change jobs. Many employees, on the other hand, are not covered by any pension plan. Government statistics from 1984 indicated that about 42 percent of the men and 30 percent of the women in the labour force were covered by employer-sponsored plans (Statistics Canada, August 1986:13), and these were mainly employees in the state sector and in more capital-intensive industries (Myles and Boyd, 1982). We might expect that many young people who are not yet established in permanent work would not belong to a voluntary pension plan and part-time or casual workers would also be unlikely to participate. If we look only at full-time workers, 58 percent of the men and 49 percent of the women belonged to pension plans, as Table 4.2 indicates. In general, pension coverage rises with age and income, but it is the low rates of coverage among low-income earners that causes most public concern.

TABLE 4.2

Proportion of Total Labour Force and
Paid Workers in the Canadian Labour Force
Covered by Pension Plans, by Sex,
1970, 1980, 1982, and 1984.

		Male	Female	Total
Percentage of	1970	37.4	28.5	34.6
Total Labour Force	1980	45.0	31.1	39.6
	1982	44.6	30.4	38.9
	1984	42.2	30.0	37.2
Percentage of all	1970	45.7	32.2	41.8
Employed Paid Workers	1980	54.0	37.6	47.6
	1982	53.6	36.2	46.5
	1984	54.4	37.1	47.0
Percentage of	1970	—	—	—
Full-time Paid Workers	1980	57.1	47.7	53.8
	1982	56.9	46.5	53.1
	1984	58.4	49.1	54.9

Source: Statistics Canada. *Pension Plans in Canada, 1984.* Cat. 74–401. Ottawa: August 1986, p. 13.

Looking at rates of pension coverage, however, does not provide the whole story of who receives pensions upon retirement. Many people contribute to plans, but because they change jobs before the pension is "vested" or legally belongs to the employee, they lose the employer's contribution and their future pension. They may be required to stay with an employer for a certain period of time (usually ten years) and to have reached a certain age (usually forty-five) before the pension belongs to the employee. If employees leave before the pension is vested, they will receive only their own contributions (if they made any), but not their employer's contribution. Since pensions are not easily "portable," they often cannot be transferred to another employer's plan, even after they are vested. Changing jobs after benefits have been vested may provide a deferred pension, but the amount of money will be much lower than for an employee who stayed with the same employer until retirement. After all, pensions are usually based on years of service and final salary (Ascah, 1984).

Some pension plans, called *money purchase plans*, pay out a benefit that is determined by the going rate for buying an annuity at the time of retirement. This means that pensions may vary considerably for people who retire at different times, even when they worked the same number of years for the same company. Annuity payments for women with similar accumulated contributions as men are generally lower because their life expectancies are longer. Since many pensions are small in the first place, and most are not protected against inflation, the amount of benefit is often nominal and insufficient to live on.

The federal government has also allowed Canadians to defer income tax by depositing savings up to a certain limit in a Registered Retirement Savings Plan at a bank or trust company. The assumption behind this scheme is that retired people will have lower incomes than when they invested in an RRSP and will not only defer income tax but will actually pay lower rates based on their lower taxable incomes after retirement. If RRSP money is withdrawn in a lump sum, it will be treated as income for taxation purposes. If it is converted to an annuity, it will be paid out monthly. With high interest rates and indexed public pensions, many older people with RRSPs have found that their taxable incomes are actually higher after retirement than when they were working. Although they may have deferred income tax, they did not avoid taxation through investment in an RRSP.

If RRSP savings have not been withdrawn by the age of seventy-one, the government requires holders to turn this money into an annuity or to place it in a Registered Retirement Income Fund (RRIF). With an annuity, the money is paid out by an insurance company on a monthly basis for a specified period of time based on the going interest rates. A RRIF, introduced in 1970, is an alternative to an annuity and allows people to control their own investments rather than giving control to an insurance company. RRIFs offer more inflation protection because they allow the individual to increase the monthly payments for the latter years of the plan when the cost of living is expected to be higher.

A coalition of senior citizens have been lobbying the government to allow more choice in retirement investments. In 1986 the federal government announced future flexibility in withdrawals from RRSP funds to allow for retirement before the age of sixty and variable interest rates for annuities. If a senior citizen is able to make use of the pension and investment deductions from income tax at $1000 each, as well as the age exemption, these tax concessions can also be of considerable assistance.

Elderly Women and Poverty

Although the elderly of both sexes receive over half their income from Canadian government pensions, unattached women rely more heavily than unattached men on these transfers. About 60 percent of the income of unattached elderly women comes from government sources compared to 46 percent for unattached elderly men (Health and Welfare Canada, 1982:12). This exemplifies the government's concern about the rising percentage of elderly Canadians — so many require financial support. Yet the poverty of senior citizens could be lessened considerably by improving pension coverage and benefits and by paying higher wages to working people, especially women.

Why are elderly women poorer than elderly men? One reason is that fewer women are in the labour force in their preretirement years — 69 percent of males aged fifty-five to sixty-four compared to 33 percent of females (Statistics Canada, 1987:84). Although most housewives worked hard raising children and maintaining the home, they received no direct pay and consequently have not contributed to CPP/QPP. They have no employer-sponsored pension, they may have few savings, and they are financially dependent on their husband's pension or family income. Although there has been some discussion of including homemakers in CPP/QPP and even providing wages for homemakers, there is lack of agreement on these issues.

A second reason for elderly women's poverty relates to women's status in the labour force. Even when women work for pay, which they are doing in increasing numbers, they are less likely than men to have private pensions or retirement savings. Despite the influx of women into the labour force since the 1950s, women are more likely than men to work in service or retail sales jobs where no employer pensions are offered. Since women often work part-time or in temporary jobs with few fringe benefits, they may never be eligible to join the company pension plan. Consequently only 30 percent of the women compared to about 42 percent of the men working in the labour force belong to employer-sponsored pension plans, and coverage rates have actually fallen slightly for both sexes since 1982 as the percentage of part-time workers has risen (Statistics Canada, August 1986:13). Because pensions are calculated as a percentage of annual income, women's work-related pensions are generally lower than men's because their incomes are only two thirds as large.

Unattached women — never-married, widowed, divorced, or separated — are the poorest among the elderly, especially those who have been widowed. Never-married women generally support themselves on their employment income, and after retirement usually have low or no work pensions. Divorced women frequently raise their children on their employment earnings and government assistance, with little or no support from former husbands. Consequently these women often cannot afford to set aside money for retirement. Widowed women sometimes expect to continue to receive their husband's work pensions, but more often than not it ceases when he dies.

In discussions on pension reform, special attention is being given to the plight of those who are not in the labour force when younger. Legislation was recently changed to ensure that more employees under federal jurisdiction will be covered by future pension plans, especially part-time employees. The contributor's years of service required to retain the employer's contribution has been lowered from ten years of service to two years of service. But if the employee leaves before the "vesting period," pension contributions need to be returned at a fair and competitive interest rate or be portable to another job.

Changing pension regulations may help solve some elderly women's poverty, but problems remain. As long as pensions are tied to a percentage of income, those with lower incomes will suffer. Legislation needs to be enforced against gender inequality in hiring, wages, promotion, and equal pay for work of equal value. This has been recommended by the federal Abella Commission on Equality in Employment (1984) and has been extensively discussed by governments. Similarly, upon marriage dissolution, the cost of rearing children needs to be divided equally between fathers and mothers. Despite the new federal divorce law, enforcing court-awarded child support continues to be a contentious issue.

Higher rates of female labour force participation, additional public day care, higher wages, and improved benefits for working women may ease some of the problems of poverty for elderly women in the future. Including homemakers in CPP/QPP, splitting pension credits upon divorce, and enforcing stricter employer pension plan coverage may also help. But as the elderly of tomorrow, younger women clearly need assistance in preparing for their retirement so that they will not become a burden to the state like so many of today's elderly women.

Pension Reform

With the aging of the Canadian population, public concern has been aroused about the potential inadequacy of public pension funds for future generations. Some people have argued that as the younger employed population becomes proportionately smaller than the dependent sector of the population, pension funds could eventually dwindle. In anticipation of this eventuality, the government announced in 1985 that CPP/QPP premiums would be raised starting January 1, 1986 from 3.8 percent of earnings to 7.6 percent by 2011. But the working population is not dwindling relative to the dependent population. Although the elderly population has increased, more women have entered the labour force, and the working population is actually growing. As a result, more employees will be available to contribute to pension plans, and this will cover the cost of indexed pensions in the future. The so-called pension "crisis" could actually be considered a political device to encourage Canadians to willingly pay higher CPP premiums.

Concern has also been expressed by women's groups and social welfare organizations that too few working Canadians are actually covered by employer-sponsored pensions. Those who change jobs frequently or work part-time are disadvantaged by vesting requirements of ten years of full-time work, still the rule in many private pensions. As a result, many groups have argued that legislation should be changed to shorten the vesting period to five or two years and to reduce the age limit, which has already been done for employers under federal jurisdiction. They have also argued that vested pensions should be portable from one employer to another. Protection against inflation is essential and a guarantee is needed that all plans will pay the same to male and female employees who retire with the same earnings record.

Others have argued that improvements to the Canadian Pension Plan would have more impact on low income groups than changes to private pension plans. Women's groups usually favour an expansion of the CPP/QPP because they feel that the plan can provide the coverage necessary to produce adequate pensions for women and men more easily than reforms to individual employee-sponsored plans. The CPP already covers most workers including part-time employees, and its benefits vest imme-diately, are portable, indexed, and cover men and women equally. The main problems with CPP are that its benefits are too low to provide an adequate income for those who must rely solely on OAS and CPP, and it does not cover those with no direct earnings (Morton, 1984:16).

Homemakers who do not work for pay have no CPP coverage except as survivors, while divorced women in this position may have no benefits at all. Treating wives as dependants of male workers ignores the contri-bution they make in raising children and performing domestic work. It also ignores the fact of divorce. For this reason, many groups, such as the National Action Committee on the Status of Women, la Fédération des femmes du Québec, the Canadian Advisory Council on the Status of Women, and the Canada Pension Plan Advisory Committee, have advo-cated a homemaker benefit in CPP.

One proposal for a homemaker's pension comes from the Report of the Parliamentary Task Force on Pension Reform in 1983. On retirement all homemakers who stayed home with children under the age of eighteen or who looked after dependent infirm adults would receive pension credits based on the number of years they worked in the home. Their earnings would be considered equivalent to half the average industrial wage. Contributions would generally be paid by the working spouse or in the case of those with low income or no spouse, contributions would be subsidized by all CPP contributors. This subsidy would involve raising premium levels again, but this was done in 1985 with little public opposition.

Controversy continues about the equity and feasibility of the home-maker's pension, and organized labour, the business community, some welfare organizations, and several women's groups have opposed it. One objection is that it disrupts the earnings-related nature of CPP. A second objection is that it benefits couples with only one wage-earner (often higher income earners) and does not acknowledge the unpaid housework performed by couples where both are in the labour force. A third objection is that it would do little to relieve women's poverty because money received from CPP would just be deducted from the Guaranteed Income Supplement, which poor elderly people already receive. And finally, some have objected that it would cost spouses and all CPP contributors too much money. Some of the organizations that object to the homemaker's pension believe that reform should focus on two-earner couples, since the one-earner family is rapidly disappearing. Increasing CPP benefits for all retired workers, splitting pension benefits upon divorce, increasing the survivor benefit, and raising women's wages upon which pension contributions are based are alternative proposals to pension reform.

Any further changes to the Canada Pension Plan would require both federal and provincial government co-operation and would be influenced by political lobby groups. The regulation of employer-sponsored pensions is predominantly a provincial matter, except in federal jurisdictions such as the public service and private retirement savings plans. But reform has been delayed because of the lack of consensus on a number of issues, such as the feasibility of a homemaker's pension and how to increase coverage under employer-sponsored pension plans. There does seem to be some consensus on the need for inflation protection and some changes are already taking place on vesting, portability, and survivor benefits.

Mandatory Retirement

In 1985 the Supreme Court of Canada ruled against the fixing of a compulsory retirement age. Later that year, a parliamentary committee on equality recommended that mandatory retirement be abolished by amending the Canadian Human Rights Act to prohibit age discrimination. Nevertheless, an Ontario Supreme Court judge ruled in October

1986 that being asked to retire from university teaching at age sixty-five is not a violation of the Canadian Charter of Rights and Freedoms. Controversy continues about whether or not older workers should be forced to retire at a specific age, and if so, what that age should be.

Mandatory retirement schemes have been defended in the past for several reasons. A set retirement age enables employees to leave their jobs without social stigma and prevents employers from having to make difficult decisions about the competence of older workers. If there were not a definite retirement age, employers might be less willing to retain older workers slightly below the present age of retirement if they were not entirely satisfied with their performance. For this reason, a fixed retirement age contains a degree of job security. Mandatory retirement also provides stability in pension systems because the timing and number of retirements can be accurately predicted in advance. The age of retirement has also been used for entitlement to social benefits such as income tax deductions, pensions, income supplements, subsidized medical services and drug plans, and reduced transit fares and entrance fees.

If mandatory retirement were abolished, on what basis would social benefits be distributed? Should people receive OAS when they are still working or should they apply for this benefit upon retirement? If the retirement age were flexible, higher income earners might be more likely to continue working while lower income earners might prefer to retire at age sixty-five. This would stigmatize the act of retirement and the receipt of the old-age pension in the way that welfare recipients are now stigmatized.

Those who favour the abolition of mandatory retirement argue that ability and not age should determine an employee's claim to a job. Jobs requiring physical strength are generally declining with technological change and most new jobs require mental rather than physical agility. Considering that average life expectancies at birth are almost eighty years for women and seventy-three years for men, many people are able to maintain their abilities well past the age of sixty-five. Furthermore, studies have found that voluntary retirees are more likely to have a positive attitude towards retirement and higher levels of satisfaction than forced retirees (Kimmel et al., 1978:575). Researchers have also found that eliminating mandatory retirement in other countries has not substantially increased the number of older workers in the labour force (Schmitt et al., 1979).

Increasing numbers of workers are opting for early retirement when given the choice, and preretirement planning is being offered by some companies as a preliminary step to relaxing retirement rules. But early retirement can also be used as an alternative to lay-offs. High youth unemployment and blocked mobility among middle-aged people can put pressure on those considering retirement, and making room for younger people is often encouraged by both employers and colleagues. In the current economic climate, however, many employers are not replacing retiring workers but are either hiring back certain retired employees on contract or increasing the workload of existing staff. Consequently whether or not an older person decides to retire may have little impact on the creation of new jobs for young people.

In 1985, despite the potential benefits of early retirement programs for job creation, the Canadian government reduced unemployment insurance benefits for older workers leaving the labour force. These changes require workers to count their severance pay, vacation pay, and pension money as income, and to exhaust these sources before receiving unemployment insurance benefits. This could discourage some workers from seeking early retirement and has certainly led to considerable controversy among those who generally retire young such as military personnel and police officers.

Retirement policies are linked with pension arrangements and any move to abolish mandatory retirement might hasten pension reform. For many unions, the solution to inadequate pension coverage and low incomes among the elderly is not to allow workers to remain in the labour force but to raise pension benefits. Although some employees would prefer working rather than receiving a larger pension, most would accept retirement close to age sixty-five (List, 1985).

The proportion of employees who wish to continue working beyond age sixty-five varies with the financial incentives, the adequacy of pension plans, the anticipated inflation, the availability of part-time or contract work, and whether the spouse is employed, in addition to other financial questions (List, 1985). Managerial workers generally choose to retire at older ages than blue-collar workers, especially those in jobs perceived as undesirable or those with periodic unemployment (Quinn, 1978; Shkop, 1982). Women often choose to retire at the same time as their husband (Baillargeon, 1982). This is another indication that growing old and retiring is not the same experience for people in differing social and economic circumstances or for men and women, as we indicated in Chapter 1. Retirement is certainly not based only on the attitudes of individuals but also depends on the availability of government or private retirement plans and the level of pension benefits (McDonald and Wanner, 1987).

In other countries, the age at which people are entitled to pensions varies from fifty-five to sixty-seven, and most countries have different ages for men and women. The reason for this differentiation is not entirely clear, but probably relates to the practice of women marrying older husbands and choosing to retire at the same time as they do. Table 4.3 shows the usual age of eligibility for pensions in various countries.

In industrialized societies, the age of retirement has declined over the last two decades with the gradual reduction of old-age poverty (James, 1985). Many people choose to retire before the established retirement age, especially if they perceive their health to be poor, dislike their jobs,

TABLE 4.3

Usual Age of Eligibility for Pension
By Country and Sex
1981

	Pensionable Age	
	Men	Women
Australia	65	60
Canada	65	65
Denmark	67	62*
France	60	60
Germany	63	63
Italy	60	55
Japan	60	55
Poland	65	60
Sweden	65	65
United Kingdom	65	60
United States	65	65
U.S.S.R.	60	55

* For single women only. For married women, pensionable age is 67.

Source: United Nations. *The World Aging Situation: Strategies and Policies.* New York: 1985, (ST/ESA/150) p. 256–7.

or feel that their retirement income will be adequate (Palmore, 1982). In Canada early retirement is more likely to be taken by single men in lower status jobs and by married women who want to retire at the same time as their husband (McDonald and Wanner, 1984). One problem with researching the issue of retirement, however, is that a variety of definitions exist for the concept of "retirement." These definitions often do not apply to self-employed people who do not receive pensions, which makes cross-cultural and cross-sex comparisons difficult (Pampel and Park, 1986). The issue is often resolved by using a self-definition as well as a reduction of working hours and receipt of social-security benefits.

In the next section we will look at the development of health insurance in Canada and the implications of population aging for Medicare.

MEDICAL INSURANCE AND HEALTH SERVICES

Medicare

Compared to many other countries, Canada's health-care system is one of the best in the world. Our national health insurance system, Medicare, was achieved in two stages. In 1957 the federal government began to share with the provinces the cost of provincially operated hospital insurance plans, but prior to this, a number of private hospital insurance plans existed. After the establishment of government hospital insurance, social and political pressure mounted for a more comprehensive health insurance. In 1964 the Royal Commission on Health Services (The Hall Commission) recommended a universal medical insurance program, and these recommendations were largely followed in the plan that was eventually established.

Since 1968 Canadians have been able to receive medical and hospital care of generally high quality regardless of their financial situation. The Medical Care Act, implemented in 1968, established a system in which the federal government provides cost-sharing grants to provincially-operated health plans. The act established the following criteria for provincial plans to obtain federal funding: (1) to cover all medical procedures by physicians and surgeons; (2) to be available to residents at all income levels; (3) to be portable from one province to another; and (4) to be operated on a non-profit basis. Although the federal government funds hospital and medical services through Medicare, each province administers its own health insurance program and medical services. This means that any special health services or drug plans for the elderly are run by the provinces.

Medicare has especially been beneficial to the poor, since health costs have risen substantially since the 1960s. The relationship between poor health and low income has been recognized by the federal government, and free or subsidized medical care has been an important part of Canada's social policy. But Medicare has also benefitted the medical profession by enabling them to receive their fees for service on a regular and reliable basis. Yet many doctors have argued that the fees set by the provincial health commissions — with the consultation of doctors, medical administrators, and the federal government — are too low and interfere with the doctor's independence as a professional.

The Medical Care Act was replaced in 1984 by the Canada Health Act. This legislation renewed the national commitment to the principles set out by the federal government, particularly the principle of universality, but it also created financial penalties for provinces that continued to allow their doctors to charge more than the established fees or their hospitals to charge user fees. These penalties have generated a lot of controversy between federal and provincial governments, and among the medical associations, hospital administrators, and provincial health ministers. However, the Canada Health Act stipulated that if extra-billing or user fees were eliminated before 1987, the amounts deducted from federal contributions to a province would be paid back. While most provinces legislated against extra-billing and user fees before or shortly after the 1984 legislation, several continued to lose federal grants by allowing these practices.

The public debate over health insurance in Canada has continued since the 1940s. Much of the controversy has related to rising costs, but concern has also been expressed over which services are included in the plan. At present, the services of nurse practitioners, midwives, and many counsellors such as psychologists are excluded from public health insurance. Heavy reliance on the services of doctors in hospitals has promoted a "curative" approach to health, which some people are trying to move away from. Expensive diagnostic tests, surgical operations, and the use of life-prolonging technology cost the taxpayer tremendous amounts of money and may yield fewer results than cleaning up the environment or improving nutrition and the standard of living (especially for native people in the North). Since these debates over priorities involve political decisions, professional jealousy, and empire building, we can only expect that they will continue.

Reforming the Health–Care System

The recent emphasis on exercise, nutrition, and regular medical checkups is an indication of a slight trend away from curative medicine. Health promotion is becoming a political issue in Canada particularly concerning environmental pollution and occupational health hazards. Air and noise pollution and stressful job situations can be legislated against, and governments are increasingly being pressured to deal with these health hazards. We now know, for example, that sidestream smoke or smoke from someone else's burning cigarette can cause lung cancer and aggravate heart problems; and that hazardous chemicals and emissions cause cancer or birth defects. Awareness of these risks has encouraged lobby groups to make a connection between the *social* causes of disease and rising health costs and to pressure governments to legislate environmental controls.

Although the Canadian health-care system is publicly-funded and universally accessible, those in urban areas have a wider variety of services at their disposal than those in more remote areas. In addition to this, several provinces charge health insurance premiums except to the poor and the elderly, but most provinces pay for health costs through federal government grants and provincial taxes. Doctors still operate on a fee-for-service basis, but the fees are established by the provincial health commission. Because health care is a provincial responsibility, Medicare consists of twelve different health insurance schemes operated by the provinces and territories, but each must adhere to federal guidelines in order to receive federal grants.

The present health-care system in Canada has been criticized because it is physician-oriented and priority is given to hospital-based procedures. The Canadian Medical Association has argued that because health services are "underfunded" by the federal government, extra-billing and user fees are necessary. However, others, such as nurses, have claimed that a lot of money is wasted in the system by using doctors for counselling and routine procedures rather than using other health professionals. Escalating costs, budget cutbacks, the closing of hospital beds, and longer delays for elective surgery have raised concerns about the future of health care in Canada. In an era of economic recession and government restraint, the federal government appears to have shifted the problem of controlling Medicare costs to the provinces by limiting grants and placing conditions on federal funding. In this way, the federal government has been able to strengthen the Medicare program while limiting its financial contribution.

In the last twenty years, health expenditures have risen dramatically in a number of countries. In Canada total health expenditures as a percentage of GNP rose from 5.6 percent in 1960 to 7.9 percent in 1981. In 1921 less than 5 percent of the Canadian population was aged sixty-five or older. By 1981, this figure had reached 10 percent and could approach 20 percent by 2031. The changing age structure is important in planning and providing health services because the elderly are the fastest growing segment of the population and are the most extensive users of health-care services. In Ontario, for example, persons aged sixty-five and over formed about 9 percent of the population in 1981 but absorbed 16 percent of physician costs and 46 percent of all institutional costs (Gross and Schwenger, 1981:123). It has been estimated that providing health care for elderly Canadians costs about 7.5 percent of the Gross National Product of $17 billion (Health and Welfare Canada, 1982). In many industrialized countries, changes need to be made to the health-care system not only to curb costs but also to improve services for an aging population.

The health problems and care needs are not uniform among the elderly, however, but vary considerably by age. Those aged eighty-five and over require the most health resources. As life expectancies rise, a greater percentage of the elderly will be eighty-five years of age and over, a fact that causes considerable concern for health administrators and governments. But some researchers have predicted that the onset of chronic illness will also rise in age, thus avoiding any "geriatric crisis" (Marshall, 1981; Fries, 1984).

Since the elderly population has increased at a time of recession and government cutbacks, however, attempts are being made to keep new expenditures to a minimum when planning facilities for them. The higher levels of institutionalization of the Canadian elderly compared to many European countries with higher proportions of people aged sixty-five and over, such as Great Britain, have been the subject of considerable research and discussion. The trend towards home care rather than institutionalization is evident in both Sweden and Great Britain, involving family members as well as paramedicals. Unfortunately, the concept of "home

Humane options for Alzheimer victims

By Jacob Reingold

Mr. Reingold is executive vice-president of the Hebrew Home for the Aged, Riverdale, N.Y., which has a special unit for Alzheimer's patients.

A Florida man's rejection of community health-care and social-service assistance, and self-reliance to the point of murdering his wife because she suffered from Alzheimer's disease, demands examination. Whatever the outcome of legal appeals, the case and public response to it in the United States raise questions about how we view the quality of long-term care for the elderly and how adequate that care is for Alzheimer's patients.

From all accounts, Roswell Gilbert, 76, was devoted to his wife, Emily, 73. He patiently told her repeatedly who she was, the year, time of day, place. He bathed and dressed her, applied her makeup, soothed her agitation and cleaned her. He relied on no one.

Finally, he killed her. Friends at the Fort Lauderdale, Fla., condominium said he couldn't stand to send his "beautiful Emily" to a nursing home, where she'd be "strapped to a bed . . . treated like a dog." He concluded their love was better served by murder than by entrusting her care to an institution. Some say there was no medical alternative. This was not so. Some say it was a mercy killing; mercy killing is not the issue.

Although her decline was irreversible, Mrs. Gilbert was not terminally ill. She ate lunch in a restaurant every day and walked around unaided with a crippling bone disorder. She might have lived five to 10 years more, her doctor told the court.

Alzheimer's was long called senility, organic brain syndrome, hardening of the arteries. Many sufferers, thought insane, were shunted into mental institutions to die. That changed in the 1960s, as deinstitutionalization released more than 300,000 psychiatric patients into U.S. communities and Medicare and Medicaid began providing funds for better therapeutic alternatives. It is clear that Alzheimer's gradual deterioration of brain cells is far different from insanity. It is not a normal part of aging.

While acute-care hospitals can do little for patients' dementia, keeping them at home without nursing help is not the solution. Because Alzheimer's warps the mind, personality and, ultimately, every mental and bodily function, it devastates families. Day by day, the victim, who must be watched around the clock, recedes into confusion, fright. There is no known cause, no cure, no way to slow the decline. No gratitude: the patient forgets what you did, who you are.

Although many North Americans do not believe it, home services, adult day care and skilled nursing facilities provide the most humane alternative for patients and families. Apparently, Mr. Gilbert never considered outside help. He suffered misguided fear that nursing home workers would physically abuse his wife.

Good nursing homes, both voluntary and propriety — especially those with Alzheimer's units — can offer care, dignity and respect to patients and respite to families.

The tragedy is not just that Mrs. Gilbert might still be alive, but that both Gilberts could have enjoyed some happiness during her final years. After anger and agitation pass, Alzheimer's patients become peaceful. They smile right to the end.

Even if Mr. Gilbert had tried to place his wife in a nursing home, it is likely a bed would not have been available. There are 1.5 million nursing home beds for an elderly population of 28 million in the United States. Cost-containment guarantees that few additional beds will be added. But the old, the chief victims of Alzheimer's, are the fastest-growing U.S. age group. By the year 2035, they will number 67 million.

Mr. Gilbert was not the first to respond to Alzheimer's with violence. So that we read no more such stories, others with Alzheimer's in the family should turn to nursing homes when available and, when not, to such aid as day-care centres, family-service agencies and home-care aides.

care" is often used as a euphemism for care by women — wives and sisters (Chappell, 1982:215). Since the organization of volunteer agencies and churches in Canada, women have provided most of the services to the elderly such as meals on wheels and home visiting services. The expectation that women will care for sick family members is one that has implicitly led them to a financially insecure old age, unless they inherited money. Ironically, the trend towards government-sponsored services and institutionalization took some of the burden of caring for the elderly away from female family members and volunteer women. Now, policies may be reversing at a time when women are entering the paid labour force and have less time and motivation for volunteer work.

In the United States there has been a proliferation of profit-oriented home health-care agencies in the past few years. This can be explained by the growing cost of health care in general, and especially the cost of institutional care. Advocates for the elderly are pressing for home-care regulation, including accreditation and monitoring (Moseley, 1986). Provincially-run Canadian nursing homes have been criticized severely for providing inadequate care to the elderly, for neglecting them, and even for physically abusing them. Lobby groups attempting to upgrade nursing home standards argue that government regulations need to be more stringent and enforcement must improve. On the other hand, nursing home owners claim that they have been operating with insufficient money and need larger grants to hire more staff and to upgrade facilities. Because women comprise the vast majority of both patients and staff in these institutions, some feminists have argued that the present condition of nursing homes in this country is a "women's issue." The low pay of workers fuels nursing home profits, but at the same time leads to resentment and possibly patient abuse by the staff (Reinharz, 1986). If wages were increased, however, many operators would be put out of business. This has led some people to argue that private nursing homes should not be allowed because they must keep their expenses low in order to make a profit and the quality of care must be secondary to this major goal.

Major reforms will have to take place in the health-care system if it is to successfully adapt to an aging population and home-centred chronic care; and the system must reflect a more encompassing definition of health care (Brunet, 1985; Chappell et al., 1986). Unfortunately, our awareness of the implications of the aging population has coincided with worldwide economic recession. Expansion of existing health facilities and services to accommodate the growing elderly population may only be possible if cutbacks are made in other parts of the health-care system. The challenge to governments and health-care administrators in Canada is to reform the system to provide better service for less money.

In a number of countries, governments have been wrestling with the same questions about how best to reduce health-care expenditures while improving services (McKenzie, 1985). In some countries, elements of the health-care system have been privatized. While a few jurisdictions have privatized only hospital food services, laundry, and cleaning, others have encouraged private clinics, hospitals, health insurance, and drug plans. Hospitals and doctors have been audited and made accountable to the public, and medical fees have been frozen. Community health centres have begun to replace the building of new centralized hospitals, and patients have been discouraged from overnight stays in hospitals by the provision of day hospitals for the chronically ill and health centres for others. Private clinics have been performing minor surgery. Central governments have not only reduced levels of funding but have also used block-funding to regional governments, leaving them to decide how these scarce resources will be allocated. Each jurisdiction has been expected to decide on different priorities so that services and facilities can be traded.

Considering the provincial jurisdiction over health care and the history of the federal Medicare system in Canada, not all of these cost-cutting measures would be palatable here. There are several, however, which seem quite feasible. One major reform already under way is a reduction in our levels of hospitalization and the building of more local clinics or community health centres. These clinics could deal with health assessment, minor surgery, counselling, and diagnostic tests; and family practitioners and medical specialists could co-operate with other health workers such as nurse practitioners, midwives, social workers, psychologists, and nutritionists. Patients could receive a variety of different health services in one building in their own neighbourhood. Such centres are already available in parts of Canada, but they could be used more extensively.

Prior to the 1960s, doctors used to make house calls. Now they are more likely to tell the patient to go to hospital emergency outside office hours or to come to their office. For some patients, especially the elderly, house calls may provide much better service. A feasibility study has been done in Halifax to assess the health of elderly people through a mobile health assessment program (Wong, Wong, and Arklie, 1985). Initial health screening was done at home by a nurse practitioner, and most patients were very happy with the service. But regular home visits by nurses and doctors could also save considerable money for chronically ill patients. If family members were paid a small wage or at least had their expenses covered by the provincial government for caring for their sick, and if doctors and other health practitioners visited patients at home, fewer new hospitals would have to be built and enormous sums of money could be saved.

Another way to improve the health of the nation and reduce medical costs would be to put more resources into preventive measures, including pollution control, occupational health and safety, nutrition, anti-smoking campaigns, and exercise facilities. Governments could take a firm stand on these issues with legislation on industrial pollution, indoor air quality, and the advertisement of cigarettes, alcohol, and "junkfood." A focus on health rather than illness could shift priorities in funding away from curative medicine in hospitals and into a variety of new fields. For example, millions of dollars could be saved by preventing automobile accidents through lower speed limits, better highways, seat belt legislation, safer cars, and less powerful vehicles. Similarly, abolishing all cigarette advertising, dropping government subsidies to the tobacco industry, and requiring cleaner indoor air in public buildings and stricter anti-pollution laws could save millions of dollars now spent treating those with lung diseases.

A focus on health rather than illness would also bring all health practitioners into the health-care system, including nutritionists, chiropractors, physiotherapists, lifestyle counsellors, midwives, and nurse practitioners. In some provinces, certain health practitioners are excluded from Medicare so that patients are forced to use physicians for many services that others could offer at much lower costs. While governments are trying to reduce health costs, physicians continue to perform many services such as lifestyle counselling, concerning nutrition, smoking, and alcohol consumption, which could be done by nutritionists and nurses. If nurse practitioners were brought into Medicare, money could be saved because they charge much lower fees than doctors. The medical profession would likely object to greater autonomy and responsibility for nurses because it would overlap their jurisdiction, yet it may become necessary to share health care among a variety of health practitioners rather than allowing one group to retain a lion's share.

Some provinces, such as British Columbia and Quebec, have attempted to redistribute health specialists, particularly doctors, to rural and northern regions by restricting urban licences or paying only partial Medicare fees to urban doctors. Some communities have tried to attract doctors and dentists with high salaries and modern facilities. Considering this situation, it is difficult to accept the Medical Association's argument that there are too many doctors. The line-ups in doctors' waiting rooms are a further indication that we do not have too many doctors from the point of view of the patient. Consequently, reducing the number of admissions to medical schools would simply reduce the occupational choices of young people and the future supply of physicians while early retirement inducements for doctors could be established to allow for new recruits into the profession.

The fee-for-service method of paying doctors is partially responsible for soaring health costs. Through this method of payment, doctors can see more patients for shorter periods of time and thereby augment their income at the public's expense. Although many Canadian doctors resist salaried work and lobby hard to maintain control over their incomes, physicians in most of Asia, southern Africa, eastern Europe, and Israel have accepted salaried work for years. In other countries, such as Italy, the Netherlands, and Great Britain, doctors have been paid by how many patients they are caring for, regardless of how often they see each patient. Public sympathy in Canada may not continue for increases in provincial fee schedules, extra-billing, or even fee-for-service for doctors, especially as workers in other occupations are losing their jobs or are seeing their wages eroded by inflation.

Decentralizing health facilities and sharing expensive equipment would also save money. The use of expensive machines to prolong the life of terminally ill or very elderly patients may be considered less acceptable as resources for health care become increasingly scarce. The dramatic rise in the cost of hospital equipment is largely responsible for the escalation of health expenditures. Once purchased, this equipment soon becomes obsolete as new models come onto the market. Necessary equipment may have to be shared, or hospitals could lease the equipment to other jurisdictions to help defray costs.

Health costs cannot continue to escalate. This simply goes against global economic reality. Workable solutions need to be found to curb these costs. Perhaps we should be looking at reducing the size of our major hospitals, curbing our "infatuation" with high technology, returning to the old-fashioned practice of home visits by doctors and other health practitioners, and relying more on community health centres that emphasize preventive health. More government resources should be allocated to public health than to acute illness and the focus should be on a healthy lifestyle. In demanding a more human approach to health and medicine, we may find that high government spending on health care does not ensure better health.

HOUSING AND COMMUNITY SERVICES

Housing Policy

In discussions about housing for the elderly, a controversy continues about whether subsidized housing should be integrated within the larger community or segregated in separate buildings or housing complexes. Most research, however, indicates that seniors prefer to live in age-homogeneous housing, where their neighbours are likely to have more in common with them and to become friends. Many seniors have negative attitudes towards young people and the noise they make and prefer to live within their own age group (Roadburg 1985:37).

Living with or even "too near" their children often makes the elderly feel dependent and incapacitated (Canadian Council on Social Development, 1973), although there are many ethnic variations in this attitude. Elderly people who live in the same building as other seniors often have more friends, are more independent, and participate in more group activities than those who live in the larger community or with their children (Sherman, 1975; McClain; 1976, Myles, 1979). Although elderly people living in nursing homes often express dissatisfaction with the regimentation, those who occupy independent apartments in the same building as other seniors express much greater satisfaction.

For some elderly people who no longer want the responsibility of caring for their own house, moving into an apartment may be preferable to staying at home, as long as they have adequate personal freedom and social contact. The inability to perform everyday tasks and loss of autonomy is very frustrating for older people and may be better solved by

Most research indicates that seniors prefer to live in age-homogenous housing. (Public Archives Canada/PA 113463)

assisting the elderly to live in senior citizen apartments rather than providing services to keep them at home. Policies to encourage deinstitutionalization in order to save money need to focus on ways of helping the elderly to retain their autonomy (Béland, 1986), but we must keep in mind that seniors are not a homogeneous group. People who live in nursing homes and senior citizen apartments do not necessarily have the same characteristics and needs as those choosing to remain in their own homes (Gutman, 1980).

The choice between building self-contained apartments or hostel accommodation with laundry, meals, and other services is often decided by providing small self-contained apartments with the option of using communal facilities for dining, laundry, and socializing. But some elderly people who move to special housing would not do so if they had inexpensive assistance in housekeeping and home maintenance. Rather than encouraging older people to move to senior citizen apartments or nursing homes to obtain their assistance, it might be cheaper for governments and seniors if visiting homemakers and nurses were provided, if special grants were available to remodel homes to make them more convenient and accessible for the elderly, and if income subsidization was upgraded to enable seniors to remain in their own homes. While such programs have existed for some time, the move towards deinstitutionalization has only recently received momentum.

The recent trend towards home care has been inspired both by economic efficiency and humanistic goals because elderly people who live at home report higher levels of satisfaction than those in institutions. But a controversy exists about whether or not home care will actually save money. Some elderly people who need services may refuse help because they fear institutionalization, and the provision of home care may reveal previously unmet needs and actually escalate costs. Service needs of the population are difficult to assess. Asking service providers or even users tends to distort the figures, since these people have a vested interest in documenting a high demand for their services (Connidis, 1981). Studies of service needs must therefore rely on random samples of the entire elderly population (Connidis, 1985).

In the last twenty years there has been an increase in the proportion of Canadians living alone, especially elderly widows. Increasing life expectancies for women have meant that more women outlive their husbands. But the construction of more rental apartments and the trends towards greater financial and psychological independence of the elderly have allowed widows to choose to live alone. Family members are still expected to care for their elderly, yet living in the same house is not considered desirable. For these reasons, the concept of a "granny flat" was devised for the temporary housing of elderly parents in the back yard of their grown-up children. Although this idea is being tried by some governments in Australia and North America, living in a small prefabricated house in the back yard is certainly not everyone's idea of a "golden age." Many elderly people prefer the independence of a senior citizens' apartment to remaining in an unmanageable house or being dependent on their children's generosity and goodwill.

The Canadian federal government provides some funds for the elderly as well as other age groups to use for subsidized housing. These grants include money to repair substandard dwellings, start-up funds for nonprofit co-operatives, and home improvement loans. They can be used by nursing homes, by senior citizen apartments, or by private individuals making changes to their home to accommodate a disabled person. Far more money, however, has been available for senior citizen homes and staff than for services to the elderly in their own homes despite the savings that could probably be made.

Community and Social Services

The federal Canada Assistance Plan provides cost-sharing with the provinces of social services for those "in need." The facilities and programs for the poor and elderly are designed and administered by the provinces and municipalities. Some examples of provincial programs for the elderly

Coalition advocates funds for home-care

A coalition of senior citizen advocacy groups wants the Ontario Government to divert funds away from institutional care into alternative housing and home-care programs.

The Ontario Coalition for Nursing Home Reform, a year-old group representing 40,000 members of 23 church, labor and community groups, based its recommendation on interviews conducted by one of its members — the United Senior Citizens of Ontario — with 1,000 senior citizens.

The survey showed that most senior citizens want to stay in their own homes and that they regard institutional care as a necessary, but unwanted, last resort.

Current provincial regulations say that to qualify for chronic home care, patients must have a medical need, a referral from a physician and a requirement for three professional visits a month, the coalition said in a statement yesterday. To be eligible for the homemaker and nurses' services program, they must have a social and financial need.

The coalition advocates that family members who keep elderly relatives at home receive tax benefits, home-renovation grants (for building a wheelchair ramp, for example) and better counselling to support their efforts.

Few options — apart from hospitals and nursing homes — exist as an alternative to home care for many elderly and disabled people, the coalition said. It called on the Ministry of Community and Social Services and the Ministry of Health to create a policy for comprehensive, universally accessible home care without a need for means tests.

The Government should build apartments with attendant care and townhouse projects that would allow senior citizens to stay at home but receive regular medical care, the group said.

The Globe and Mail, February 14, 1985.

include homemakers' services, day-care programs for the chronically ill, transportation services for the elderly, seniors centres, extended-care hospitals, senior citizens' drug plans, exemption from health insurance premiums, and special discounts for recreational facilities and services.

New Horizons was established in 1972 by Health and Welfare Canada to promote the social participation of older adults. Non-profit projects are funded that are organized and run by the seniors themselves. The

type of projects sponsored include sports, recreation, and crafts programs; historical, educational, and cultural projects; social services; information services; and activity centres. In order to apply for a New Horizons
grant, a group of at least ten persons, most of whom are older and
permanently retired, must agree to serve as voluntary project directors.
Funds are not available for salaries but may be granted for capital
expenditures.

The National Advisory Council on Aging was formed in 1980 by the
Minister of Health and Welfare to counsel the minister on matters relating
to the quality of life of the aged and to stimulate public discussion on
issues relating to aging. The council consists of appointed members from
across the country with a secretariat and budget provided by the Department of Health and Welfare. In 1981 an Office on Aging was established
within the Department of Health and Welfare. The goals of the office
are to gather and provide information on the elderly and to act as liaison
between government departments and voluntary agencies dealing with
aging.

New Drug Law

*Legislation that will help lower the cost of prescription drugs to
Ontario residents was introduced in November by Health Minister
Murray Elston. The Ontario Drug Benefit Act and the Prescription
Drug Cost Regulation Act are designed to protect all consumers of
prescription drugs in the province.*

*"The Ontario Drug Benefit Act will continue to ensure that
elderly people receive high quality prescription drugs without charge,
and it will allow the government to expand the Ontario Drug
Benefit program to include essential new drugs," Mr. Elston said.*

*The Ontario Drug Benefit plan cost $350 million last year, com-
pared to $100 million six years earlier. One of the major factors
contributing to these rapidly rising costs has been the artificially
high prices of many drugs listed in the ODB Formulary, and the
new legislation will help restore prices to realistic levels.*

*"The new drug pricing legislation is part of the government's
commitment to all citizens of this province, and it will ensure that
they receive their drugs at the most reasonable cost," Mr. Elston
said.*

"It will also help consumers be better informed."

Ontario Advisory Council on Senior Citizens, 1986.

Municipal and Non–Governmental Benefits

In addition to federal and provincial programs for the elderly, municipal governments, the private sector, and voluntary organizations provide benefits for particular groups of elderly people. In comparison to federal and provincial benefits, the magnitude of these benefits is small, yet they should nevertheless be acknowledged (McKenzie and Stilborn, 1985).

Many employers provide pension plans for their employees, which are the most important non-government benefit. Over one half of private sector and nearly all public sector plans are contributory, with the employee as well as the employer paying into the plan. However, nearly one half of private sector plans are non-contributory and provide non-portable pensions more similar to pure benefits (Statistics Canada, August 1986:17). The participation rates in private pension plans vary from occupation to occupation, ranging from a low rate for agricultural workers (1 percent) to over half for those working in manufacturing, transportation, and communications.

Corporations and municipal governments also offer discounts to senior citizens. Transportation companies provide fare reductions; some universities, colleges, and vocational schools waive tuition fees; museums, art galleries, and theatres often reduce regular admission fees; and banks sometimes offer special rates and services to seniors. Reductions in fares and increased services to the elderly are often attempts to increase the participation rates in commercial, entertainment, or transportation services and are certainly viewed as favourable publicity.

Voluntary organizations provide an extensive range of services to the elderly, particularly in urban areas. These include services such as day care for the chronically ill, home nursing care, alcohol and drug dependency treatment, and homemakers' assistance. These services are financed by charitable donations and in some cases government subsidies.

Special government programs and services for the elderly have been politically popular in Canada despite the financial cost. Since we will all be old some day, we may actually benefit from many of these services and therefore are willing to have our tax dollars invested in this area. In comparison to other industrialized countries, however, Canada's social-security programs for the elderly have been criticized for providing inadequate income for the elderly poor. In the next section we will look at some of these comparisons.

AN INTERNATIONAL COMPARISON OF PROGRAMS FOR THE ELDERLY

Among the contemporary capitalist democracies, expenditures for the elderly form the largest component of the welfare-state budget (Myles,

1984:2). Old-age pensions and benefits to survivors, widows, and the disabled constitute up to 80 percent of the income maintenance programs in some OECD countries. In Canada this figure was about 40 percent in 1972 (Myles, 1984:18,19), but had risen to over 50 percent by 1984 (Health and Welfare Canada, 1985).

In *Old Age and the Welfare State*, John Myles attempts to explain qualitative differences in public pension systems of capitalist democracies. He argues that the critical factor accounting for differences in pension entitlements is the involvement of the working class in the political process and the election to office of working class parties (Myles, 1984:98). In addition, a highly competitive, democratic electoral process increases the responsiveness of parties to the demands of the electorate. Yet these factors can only be effective within certain economic conditions. Public pension systems expanded in the decades after World War II, but since the mid-seventies expansion has come to a virtual standstill in most capitalist democracies.

Comparing programs for the elderly in different countries is not an easy exercise because of variations in the cost of living and the fact that the relative importance of national, regional, and local benefits may also vary. In addition, a comparison of the monetary value of programs may ignore other benefits such as subsidized housing and transportation, food stamps, or free health care. In some countries, pensioners receive both a universal and an earnings-related benefit.

Basic pension benefits are usually inadequate without other resources and most countries augment them for those in financial need. The comparative adequacy of pensions has been calculated by relating them to the national average wage or looking at pensions as a percentage of preretirement income. Using either of these two methods, Canadian and American pensions are low relative to countries such as Sweden, France, and West Germany (OECD, 1976; United Nations, 1985). An American study of twelve industrialized countries showed that the old-age pension benefit level available to an average worker in the manufacturing industry in 1980 ranged from 29 percent to 69 percent of the previous year's earnings for a single beneficiary and from 47 percent to 83 percent of the previous year's earnings for a couple (Aldrich: 1982:5). In Canada the replacement rate in 1980 was 34 percent for a single worker and 49 percent for a couple; one of the lowest of the twelve countries. The United States was 44 percent and 66 percent in the same year.

Compared to other parts of the world and especially developing countries, however, elderly Canadians and Americans financially are very well-off. In developing countries, newly introduced social-security schemes for the elderly were generally designed to cover all categories of the wage-earning population. But in fact they are sometimes limited to specific categories of workers. Expansion to other categories of workers has often been slower than expected, with coverage sometimes limited to urban

TABLE 4.4

Replacement Rates of Social Security Old-Age Pensions for Workers with Average Wages in Manufacturing, and for Couples, Selected Countries, 1969–80

	Pension as % of earnings in year before retirement					
	Single Worker			Aged Couple		
	1969	1977	1980	1969	1977	1980
Austria	67	64	68	67	64	68
Canada	24	33	34	41	47	49
Denmark	31	27	29	45	44	52
France	41	64	66	56	78	75
Federal Republic of Germany	55	54	49	55	54	49
Italy	62	64	69	62	64	69
Japan	26	53	54	27	57	61
Sweden	42	59	68	56	73	83
Switzerland	28	39	37	45	59	55
United Kingdom	27	28	31	43	43	47
United States	30	40	44	44	60	66

Source: *Social Security Bulletin*, vol. 45, no. 11, November 1982, p. 5.

industrial workers, civil servants, military personnel, and teachers. The majority of the labour force who are rural workers and self-employed persons remain unprotected. In these countries social security fails to effectively protect the neediest workers and their families (United Nations, 1985:84,85).

Although the percentage of elderly people in the total population in developing countries is lower than in industrialized countries, the sheer number of elderly people is large and growing rapidly. In Third World countries, most elderly people live with their families, providing essential services such as housework and child care. But families clearly need assistance, especially in caring for the sick or dependent elderly, as incomes are low and two wage-earners are often needed to support the family. Before adequate policies and programs for the elderly can be devised, however, basic problems such as impure water, widespread poverty, chronic disease, food shortages, and low wages need to be addressed. Economic and cultural dependency, which characterizes many Third World nations, needs to be considered when outside advisors and consultants assist in designing and developing programs for the elderly (Neysmith and Edwardh, 1984).

In China, where social services and pensions are not well developed, the family is expected to care for the sick, the handicapped, and the elderly. China, as well as Germany, has actually written this obligation into legislation. According to the 1980 Marriage Law in China, children must look after and support their parents when they are no longer able to work and care for themselves. This will certainly place increased pressure on the family in the future because family size is declining. The one-child policy, which is enforced through tax and financial incentives, will place a heavier burden on children. If the one-child policy is effective, who will care for the elderly in thirty years? It may be necessary to create more state-funded facilities and services for the elderly, whose numbers grow larger as the birth rate falls (Clarfield and Paltiel, 1986).

In many countries work and retirement policies are inflexible, forcing older workers to choose between economic hardship and continuing to work beyond the retirement age. Forced retirement can lead to feelings of social isolation and lack of social participation as well as a sudden drop in income. But staying in the labour force can cause hardships for younger workers seeking employment or promotion; for employers who often prefer younger, more adaptable employees; and for older employees who are pressured into working full-time when they may not have the motivation or energy.

Inequalities exist in the old-age benefits available to men and women in many countries. Because of their limited access to paid work, women often find themselves with no coverage upon reaching old age. Even when they are in the labour force, interruptions for childbearing make it difficult to accumulate sufficient periods of insurance to qualify for normal old-age pensions. Lower wages than men also lead to lower benefits, since social-insurance benefits are usually related to previous wages. Throughout the world, women are among the most impoverished sectors of the elderly population, and considering women's faster-rising life expectancies, governments will need to address this problem. Part-time and migrant workers are also frequently caught outside the income security system upon old age.

Another issue with income security centres on the impact of worldwide inflation and rising energy costs on the limited incomes of the elderly (United Nations, 1985). While a number of industrialized countries have tried to maintain the purchasing power of pensions in recent decades, there remains a need to strengthen provisions for indexing pensions in programs around the world. Plans for future social-security programs must take into consideration projections of the population, especially dependency ratios. Policy-makers need to be aware of the potential burden placed on future generations of wage-earners when designing new pension schemes.

CONCLUSION

Retirement policies and benefits for the elderly have only been possible in those societies with enough surplus to afford them. In many industrialized countries, benefits for the elderly increased substantially after World War II when production increased and labour markets expanded. In some developing nations, however, the best that can be provided is a pension for certain categories of state employees or urban workers. Those outside these job or residential categories must provide for their own retirement, which means that retirement remains a luxury for wealthier people.

The trend towards earlier retirement continues in industrialized countries despite rising life expectancies. This trend is accompanied by an attempt to eliminate sex discrepancies in the age of retirement and in benefits and to come closer to maintaining preretirement incomes. In many countries old-age pensions are increasingly perceived as a right rather than a privilege and are no longer focused solely on the poor.

In the final chapter we will argue that the way a particular cohort ages in the future is influenced by when and how they experience certain stages in the life cycle. These stages are less distinct than they were thirty years ago. Rather than finish school, enter the work force, marry, raise children, see the children leave home, and retire, more people will marry, remarry, and perhaps start a second family. They may return to school at an older age and change careers or jobs several times. Any predictions about the service needs and lifestyles of the future elderly must take into consideration the heterogenity of Canadian society as well as the ways in which present trends in education, family formation, labour force participation, life expectancy, mobility, and lifestyles may influence patterns of aging in years to come.

5

THE FUTURE ELDERLY

INTRODUCTION

In order to make predictions about the future elderly, it is necessary to understand a number of demographic and social changes from the past few decades. We are making the assumption that people born in a particular cohort are likely to be influenced as they age by changes such as rising divorce rates, declining fertility, reconstituted families, non-legal marriages, and more women in the labour force. Stone and Fletcher (1987) made similar assumptions when they analysed the probabilities of men and women experiencing certain "living arrangement passages" at various ages. Changing living arrangements such as marrying at a certain age or divorcing are typical of particular cohorts, but not others. In this chapter we will begin by discussing some of the changes in what we call "life transitions" and their potential implications for the aging process, and then use the baby-boom generation as a target group to make some predictions about the future elderly.

CHANGES IN LIFE TRANSITIONS

With past demographic trends and the rising cost of supporting children and the elderly, our images of various life transitions and stages have changed. In times of high infant mortality and child labour, parents could not afford the luxury of becoming too sentimental about childhood. Similarly, when children were expected to enter the work force as soon as they could help support the family, adolescence as a separate stage of life was virtually non-existent. Before compulsory retirement and the development of old-age social security, old age could not be seen as a period of leisure unless the community or family had a surplus of money to support the elderly. When those too old to work were dependent on their children for their existence, growing old was seen as an inevitable but unfortunate event.

Since the decline in infant mortality, the abolition of child labour, the development of compulsory retirement, and the establishment of old-age social security designed to replace wages, both childhood and old age have increasingly been seen as stages of leisure, free from the responsibility of earning a living. In the same way that our images of childhood, adolescence, middle age, and old age have been transformed in the past, future demographic, economic, and social changes will continue to alter how we view the aging process and different stages of life.

Children in industrial society are increasingly segregated from adults through compulsory schooling and age-homogeneous recreational activities. This physical segregation probably creates social distance as well, making it more difficult to understand the lifestyles of those in another generation. With the extension of higher education to a greater proportion of the population, youth dependence on family has been prolonged. But with high unemployment rates, young people are pressured to stay at school even longer and to continue to live with their parents simply because they cannot find full-time work. While the expansion of part-time work has granted students some measure of independence, it has not allowed them to be self-supporting. Becoming an adult is usually marked by financial independence from family and the formation of a separate household. Many young people are now frustrated because they feel they have the maturity to act responsibly and independently, but not the opportunity to show their abilities or make a useful contribution to society.

As more couples live together before marriage, the significance of the wedding day as the beginning of sexual experience and adult responsibility is weakened. Yet many of these couples eventually marry. Even after living together for years, many brides and grooms cling to the traditional ceremonies and symbols of marriage because our society has not created adequate alternatives to acknowledge their prior relationships. The white wedding dress symbolizing virginity is part of a rite of passage, even for the bride who has previously lived with the groom. Although marriage ceremonies can be changed and there is no requirement to marry in a church, for the bride to wear white, for the bride's father to "give her away," or for guests to throw fertility symbols (confetti), many people still go through these traditional motions for lack of an established alternative or love of tradition itself.

Marriage and child birth are usually occasions for family celebration, but we still provide no formal training for the responsibilities these entail. While educational requirements for most paid jobs have increased, and while the state has become more involved with many aspects of our personal lives, the only preparation needed for marriage is an inexpensive licence. Despite the fact that raising children has become increasingly demanding in the two-income family, young people remain far less prepared for domestic responsibilities than for their paid work lives.

In spite of the attention paid to low birth rates and childless marriages, most people still choose to marry and bear children. About 93 percent of Canadians marry at some point in their life and about 93 percent of married women bear children (Gee, 1987). Although slightly more women now remain childless by choice, this increase is not statistically large because it is offset by lower rates of involuntary childlessness (Veevers, 1980). Advances in medical technology have enabled most women who choose to have children to become pregnant.

Living together before marriage has become a form of courtship that is gaining acceptance among young people, but freer attitudes towards sex have altered relationships among people of all ages. Living together without legal marriage is especially typical of the formerly married, who may be wary of the institution or not legally free to remarry. But this permissiveness has also triggered a demand for more legal protection of individuals outside marriage. It is now possible to live a full life outside of marriage and even to produce and rear children without a permanent partner. But we will have to wait and see how this new lifestyle affects children as they grow older and parents as they age.

Few social scientists have studied the nature of adult development, although governments gather statistics on numerous aspects of adult life such as marriage, birth rates, divorce, labour force participation, unemployment, and home ownership. While some studies have been made of adult life transitions and mid-life crises (Sheehy, 1974; Levinson, 1978), social scientists have largely neglected middle age as a research topic and have chosen instead to analyse the stages of development in childhood or old age. Because of the assumption that personality and lifestyle were usually stable in middle age, this stage of life was seen as less interesting. But we now know that the socialization process continues throughout the life span and that people's attitudes and behaviour often change with life transitions such as marital disruption and occupational changes. These new understandings and trends should trigger more research of mid-life and of the implications that marital disruption, remarriage, or job changes have for older people.

With higher rates of marriage dissolution and remarriage, sexual activity among the middle-aged and elderly is now more frequently acknowledged. While people often find it difficult to imagine their older parents engaged in sexual activity, it is easier to imagine an older "courting" couple so involved. Yet we still tend to associate sex with youth and beauty. Changing lifestyles, however, make it increasingly difficult to assume that unmarried or older people are celibate.

The growing tendency for married women with young children to work for pay has many implications for family relationships, for legal and social change, and for elderly women. Today's women are less often forced to make a choice between childbearing and paid work than in the past. This fact has not only affected their willingness to stay in an unsatisfactory marriage, but it has created greater financial and emotional independence for women, which undoubtedly will continue into old age. Although women's wages are often low and fewer women than men belong to employer-sponsored pension plans, today's working women will be more likely than their mothers to reach old age without total financial dependence on either their husbands or the government. In addition, depression and lack of purpose in life when the children leave home is less of a problem for today's working mothers than for the generation that exclusively focused their lives around their family.

Despite changes in women's roles, different connotations are still placed on the aging process of men and women. Men are perceived to be more experienced, knowledgeable, expert, and wealthy with age while aging for women is still associated with loss of attractiveness, sexuality, and relationships. As the baby-boom generation ages and more consumers are older women, however, business people stand to gain from acknowledging the presence of elderly people and especially older women as clients and consumers with special interests. Changes in this direction are already noticeable in advertising for the clothing industry, hotels, airlines, and automobiles, where business women and seniors have become the new target groups for sales. The future elderly, moreover, could form a powerful pressure group for many marketing changes such as smaller-sized packaging, larger print on labels, home delivery of groceries, and special holiday packages.

While retirement used to be seen as the beginning of old age at least for men, flexible retirement policies will make the transition less abrupt in the future. In the nineteenth century aging implied a gradual winding down of work activities. This may again become the pattern as some workers opt for part-time work before accepting full-retirement. At the same time, retirement from work will become more consequential to women. Those who can afford to retire early may engage in travel, consulting work, volunteer work, or leisure activities while those with fewer resources will have to remain working. Although early retirement was viewed as progressive only a decade ago, it is now seen as expensive because it requires larger pension funds (James, 1985).

Retirement planning and courses are increasingly being offered by employers. New policies of having older employees work two or three days a week and receive partial pension benefits for the remainder of the week have been tried in England, France, and Sweden and are being considered in Canada. This gradual form of retirement may lessen the financial and psychological costs to the older worker and at the same time provide job vacancies for younger workers. Yet rules for pension benefits must be changed in order to allow gradual retirement, since benefits are usually based on the highest years of income and these are generally the last few before retirement.

 The elderly have become increasingly segregated through compulsory retirement, senior citizen clubs, and retirement villages, but this trend may be slowed down by more flexible retirement policies and the increased

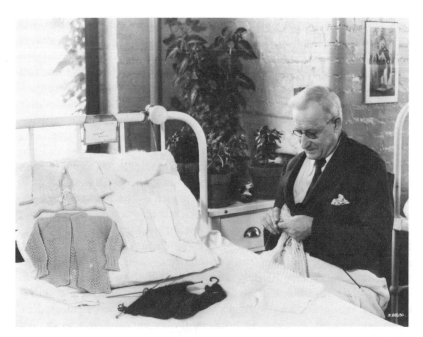

The elderly have become increasingly segregated through compulsory retirement, senior citizen clubs, and retirement villages. (Public Archives Canada/PA 60538)

political presence of older people in voluntary organizations. However, while the elderly in industrialized countries are living longer, retiring earlier, and experiencing more leisure time, the elderly in developing countries are still expected to contribute to the family income until the end of their lives if they come from the poorer segments of their society. Retirement and leisure in these countries remains a luxury for the rich.

Demographic, economic, and policy trends influence the way we treat children, adolescents, and older people. Our social rituals often reflect this treatment, but generally lag behind the trends. No longer do we consider a boy to be a man at the age of thirteen, although some religions still ritualize the coming of age at this time. Similarly, we may no longer automatically think of ourselves as old when we retire from work or receive a pension. With an aging population and longer life expectancies, we are beginning to rethink past policies, practices, and attitudes about aging and life transitions.

COMPARISON BETWEEN PRESENT AND FUTURE ELDERLY

Today's Elderly

The generation of Canadians now aged sixty-five and over have grown old in a different social and economic world than the elderly of the future will. Today's elderly grew up and reached adult life without the assistance of the many social-security programs available today. When they were younger, social roles were more rigid and lifestyles less flexible. For example, people generally married, had children, raised them, and watched them grow more independent. Although many families experienced the death of a child or spouse and some experienced desertion, married people generally counted on marital stability. They aimed for financial security, home ownership, and a better life for their children. They engaged in a certain amount of vicarious living through their children, but did not anticipate much self-development outside of family life. Married women were expected to be homemakers, men breadwinners.

Many of today's elderly were greatly affected by the 1930s Depression and the Second World War. The Depression may have curtailed their education, delayed their marriage, or forced them to accept work that was secure rather than interesting. Trying to make ends meet during those years encouraged both thrift and financial anxiety. Going overseas to war may have been the only opportunity for some young people to find work, travel, and see the world, as well as serve their country. However, many surviving veterans and their families were changed by the experience of wartime destruction, the death of their friends and families, shortages of food, loneliness, and personal disability. Both the Depression and the Second World War undoubtedly made a lasting impression on today's elderly, affecting their attitudes, expectations, and behavioural patterns.

Today's elderly needed to be prepared for the unexpected in life, perhaps more than the postwar generation. In their earlier years, today's elderly did not have reliable birth control, social insurance programs, income support benefits, or as much state protection in their personal lives. Many prepared themselves psychologically for potential problems by cultivating an attitude of resignation or a belief in "God's will." Others were able to save money for future crises or to form a network of supportive friends and relatives who were willing to help out if necessary. Many of today's elderly relied on their family for assistance, especially their children whom they hoped would feel a reciprocal responsibility and would care for them in their old age.

Social Security and the Postwar Generation

Those born in the postwar period — the baby-boomers — have been raised to take government social programs for granted. They were brought up to assume that Family Allowances would help to pay for their own childhood expenses and for their future children's expenses. They assumed that hospital and medical insurance would cover most of their health-care costs. Unemployment and disability insurance would protect them if they could not find work, if they were injured, or if they needed time off for childbearing. When they grow older, they will continue to count on government benefits like Old Age Security and Medicare.

The postwar generation was not only raised on social security but also on a variety of private insurance policies and benefits. Some have purchased life insurance policies, private disability insurance, insurance on all their possessions, and contributed to an employer-sponsored pension plan or a registered retirement savings plan. While this generation is unlikely to have accumulated substantial savings because they tend to live for the present and buy "on time," they often feel that they can count on government benefits or their credit cards to carry them through hard times.

The baby-boomers have also come to take inflation for granted. The assumption that land and houses will rise in value has encouraged them to see these as investments for their future. The assumption that paycheques will rise each year and in some cases that social benefits will be indexed to the rising cost of living has led to the practice of living for the present and not worrying too much about accumulating "emergency money" for the future. The widespread use of credit cards means that many Canadians are actually in debt rather than accumulating money for their old age. In addition, many see retirement from work with a pension as a "right" rather than a privilege. Some look forward to early retirement and more leisure time but do not anticipate a substantial drop in income because, in fact, some of their parents are actually richer in their retirement.

Many middle-class baby-boomers have grown up watching their parents scrimp and save for their retirement only to find that their parents now have more money than they ever anticipated. Indexed pensions, increased government benefits, and rising interest rates that augmented their savings have made their elderly parents' lifestyle much more comfortable than expected. This situation can lead the younger generation to solidify their desire to live in the present and not to worry about the future. On the other hand, those from poorer families may have watched their parents struggle on government pensions, with few personal savings or investments. Rather than encouraging the younger generation to save more money for their old age, this observation may lead them to expect better employer-sponsored and government pensions in the future and to be more willing to fight for higher benefits and greater coverage. The idea of social insurance and employment fringe benefits is well entrenched in the psyche of the postwar generation and has affected their outlook on the future.

Family Structure and Gender Roles

With inflation and high interest rates, the two-income family has become an economic necessity for many families. But the dual-income family has also enabled young couples to live more comfortably than their parents did. However, inflated mortgage rates and rents, the extra labour-saving devices, the clothes required when wives work full-time, the need for two cars, and paid child care all raise family expenses. Although most wives work because they have to economically, the dual-income family has increased our standard of living and raised expectations for material goods. Some researchers have argued that the dual-income family is one factor that has increased the gap between rich and poor families (Wolfson, 1986). One-parent families, most often led by women, are often poor and continue to be poor in comparison to the "typical" Canadian family, which now has two incomes.

Fewer mothers now stay home to care for their own children, and this may eventually lead to changes in the division of labour in families. Although most wives still retain responsibility for the housework and after-hours child care even when they work full-time for pay (Meissner et al., 1975; Clark and Harvey, 1976; Luxton, 1980; Armstrong and Armstrong, 1983), greater participation in housework by husbands is inevitable given the stresses on women of a double workload (de Koninck, 1985). In the future, elderly men could benefit from this added responsibility when they retire or are widowed. At the present time, lack of domestic skills and lack of intimacy with their children have led to dependence and loneliness among some older men who were brought up with more segregated gender roles.

Today's high divorce rates will undoubtedly have an impact on tomorrow's elderly. In the United States nearly 60 percent of children will experience divorce in their families before they are eighteen years old (Reed, 1986). Most of these children will continue to live with their mothers on drastically reduced incomes. The lower standard of living for divorced wives compared to husbands largely results from reformed laws that ignore the actual inequalities inherent in most marriages (Weitzman, 1985). High divorce rates and the phasing out of alimony force women into the labour force where they can seldom earn comparable incomes to their former husbands and consequently seldom accrue adequate pension credits for their retirement. Divorce could also alienate children from one set of grandparents, and remarriage of their parents could give children three sets of grandparents.

Although the divorce and remarriage rates are lower in Canada, some people now experience two or even three marriages in their lifetime. Unlike remarriage after widowhood, former spouses still exist and could continue to make their presence felt, which could add stress to reconstituted families. Divorced men, who are likely to remarry younger women, could quite feasibly have two sets of children, the second much younger than the first. Upon retirement, a man could have an ex-wife similar to him in age and a present wife still in the labour force. Remarriage not only complicates kin relations but also pension and survivor benefits. If

TABLE 5.1

Total Fertility Rates*
from 1971 to 1996, Canada

Observed

1971	2.19
1976	1.82
1981	1.70

Projected**

1986	1.60
1991	1.50
1996	1.40

* average number of births per woman during her childbearing years
** assuming present trend continues

Source: Statistics Canada. *Population Projections for Canada, Provinces and Territories 1984–2006.* Cat. 91–520. Ottawa: Supply and Services, May 1985, p. 22.

CPP credits are split upon divorce, which wife and which set of children are entitled to benefits? Although women may benefit from pension-splitting, will men be able to live on reduced pensions that are already relatively low?

Lower fertility rates will also have an impact on the lives of the future elderly, as Table 5.1 indicates. The postwar generation of women are spending less of their lives raising children; and as these parents age, fewer children will be available to care for their parents when they can no longer care for themselves. High rates of job mobility may take children far away from their parents, leaving community organizations, government services, and hired caretakers to fill the gap made by the absence of relatives. The future generation of elderly, however, may be much more independent from family than today's elderly. With fewer children, they may have developed more extensive friendship networks and may be more used to purchasing services. New facilities and services will undoubtedly be developed by government, community groups, and private enterprise as the population ages and their needs become more apparent.

As life expectancies rise (see Table 5.2), older people may be more likely to live to see their great grandchildren grow up. Although each woman may bear fewer children, it is possible that more generations will be available to assist the elderly. Alternatively, fewer children may place an increasingly heavy burden on middle-aged women who have traditionally been responsible for family health and integration. Women, who

TABLE 5.2

Life Expectancy at Birth for Males and Females in Canada, 1976 to 1996

	Female	Male
Observed		
1971	76.4	69.3
1976	77.5	70.2
1981	79.0	71.9
Projected		
1986	80.0	72.9
1991	80.8	73.9
1996	81.6	74.9

Source: Statistics Canada. *Population Projections for Canada, Provinces and Territories 1984–2006*. Cat. 91–520. Ottawa: Supply and Services, May 1985, p. 27.

As life expectancies rise, it will not be unusual to find living representatives of three generations within one family. (Photograph by Harold M. Lambert/Miller Comstock Inc.)

themselves may be working full-time, could retain responsibility for their aging parents, their mature children (especially if they experience divorce or unemployment), and at the same time be expected to be enthusiastic grandparents. The too-heavy burden on women of this generation may force improvements in public facilities and services for the elderly or shift more responsibility to male family members.

Employment

The baby-boom generation has much more formal schooling than today's elderly. This increased education is often equated with higher aspirations for promotion and income, as well as longer life expectancies and increased satisfaction in retirement. Despite high unemployment rates and blocked mobility in career positions, adolescents still expect to go to college or university and anticipate financial rewards for their diplomas and degrees (Baker, 1985). Many young adults have been able to obtain higher status jobs than their parents and to have a more affluent lifestyle because of post-secondary education. Others simply earn more money than their parents ever earned but are also more willing than their parents' generation to spend this money on travel, cars, clothing, or entertainment.

Technological change could raise individual productivity and maintain high levels of unemployment in the future (Messinger and Powell, 1987). Both high unemployment and technological change imply that fewer people will have one major job or career for life, but rather will experience several job transitions, career changes, and periods of retraining. Movement between jobs or from employee to self-employed status will necessitate more portable employer-sponsored pension plans and greater investment in registered retirement savings plans. The traditional middle-class pattern of education, work, promotion, and retirement is already being disrupted with more middle-aged people returning to school and changing jobs or careers in mid-life. If birth rates continue at their present low levels, we may actually experience a shortage of labour in certain skilled labour occupations and there may therefore be a greater demand for older workers in these occupations. At the same time, however, new technological firms may hire mainly young people and move beyond the border to find recruits with the specified technical education.

The trend for earlier retirement will continue as long as public pensions are indexed and private pension coverage is extended to more employees. Those with higher status jobs, however, may choose to stay in the labour force longer because they receive more personal satisfaction from their work than those with lower status jobs. As a result, more employers may want to offer incentives for higher status employees to retire at younger ages. Changes to the Canada Pension Plan now allow greater flexibility in retirement age and those who retire later can draw higher pensions.

Provincial governments now need to change their pension laws to enable more people to retire with adequate benefits.

Health

Although researchers are still arguing about the future health needs of elderly people, improved health coverage, better nutrition, and more extensive income support programs will undoubtedly affect the health of the future elderly. Fewer Canadians should experience disabilities from malnutrition, from childhood diseases such as polio, or from war injuries in the future. There will probably continue to be high rates of cancer, heart disease, smoking-related ailments, and disabilities from pollution and motor vehicle accidents, however. Since Medicare was established in the 1960s, poverty has become less of a barrier to curative health than it used to be. Even though the gap in life expectancies between rich and poor will still be apparent, the effects of state medicine will probably begin to reduce the gap.

Present trends towards a more healthful diet, more exercise, and less cigarette smoking may also improve the health of the future elderly compared to the present elderly. But Canada's health-care system will have to adopt a broader definition of health and will be forced to deemphasize the present focus on institutional care by doctors and curative illness to accommodate the growing number of elderly people with chronic ailments.

CONCLUSION

The status of elderly people has changed with the age distribution of the population and the economic, social, and political contributions each group has made to the society. Social norms associated with aging and relations between the generations have also varied in different historical time periods and among cultural and socio-economic groups. When families, communities, or societies have a surplus of food or money, the very young and the very old can be exempted from productive labour. But only since the Second World War have governments and employers in industrialized countries promoted retirement from work by providing more adequate social-security benefits and pensions for the elderly. Without adequate social benefits, retirement is not possible for most of the population.

With the aging of the baby-boom generation, social benefits, facilities, and services for the elderly will have to be expanded at greater cost to the Canadian taxpayer. But we can expect little public resistance to expanding services and facilities, since we have now come to rely on these benefits. Because we all grow old and many of us worry about old age, we are willing to pay the price of providing for the future elderly. By the time the baby-boom generation reaches the end of its life span, we may see a surplus in public pension funds once again and find empty nursing homes like the elementary schools of the 1980s. In the meantime, financing pensions and health care for the growing proportion of elderly people remains an important political priority in many industrialized nations.

Despite the concern about population aging in industrialized nations, most developing nations' social programs are still preoccupied with reducing birth rates and providing food and schooling for large numbers of children. Life expectancy at birth in these countries is low by North American standards, yet many people live as long as we do. Although population aging is becoming a problem for Third World countries, few of these nations have the resources to offer old-age pensions or other benefits for the elderly. The proportion of elderly people may be lower than in industrialized countries, but the sheer numbers of elderly people in developing nations are very high and growing (Neysmith and Edwardh, 1984; United Nations, 1985).

The aging of the North American population has been accompanied by a growing interest in the social policy aspects of aging. As a social and economic policy issue, the aging population has stimulated considerable research, but social gerontology still remains a developing field in terms of theory and comparative analysis. Much more research is needed to compare aging in developing and industrialized countries and among different cultural groups and social classes. We also need to understand how the elderly lived in various historical periods before we can appreciate the process of growing old, the variables influencing policy for the elderly, and what it means to be elderly in different social contexts.

Canadian politicians and policy-makers are planning for the service needs of future elderly people. Before such decisions are made, however, they need to know what researchers have discovered about how attitudes and behaviour vary with age, and how and why relations between the elderly and other groups have changed over time. But policy-makers also need a sound knowledge of social science or advice from outside experts. Our hope is that the research and theories discussed in this volume will introduce students to the topic, assist them to become more knowledgeable about aging and the elderly, and perhaps even encourage them to pursue their studies in order to make some future impact on social policy relating to elderly persons.

BIBLIOGRAPHY

Abu-Laban, Sharon McIrvin. "The Family Life of Older Canadians."
 Canadian Home Economics Journal, January 1978, pp. 16–25.

Abu-Laban, Sharon, and Abu-Laban, Baha. "Women and the Aged as
 Minority Groups. A Critique." *Canadian Review of Sociology and
 Anthropology* 14, no. 1 (1977): 103–116.

Achenbaum, W. Andrew. *Old Age in the New Land: The American
 Experience Since 1790.* Baltimore: John Hopkins Press, 1978.

Adams, O.B., and Lefebvre, L.A. *Retirement and Mortality.* Ottawa: Statistics
 Canada, 1980.

Adler, H.J., and Brusegard, D.A., eds. *Perspectives Canada III.* Ottawa:
 Statistics Canada, 1980.

Aldrich, Jonathon. "Earnings Replacement Rate of Old-Age Benefits in 12
 Countries, 1969–80." *Social Security Bulletin* 45, no. 11 (1982):
 3–11.

Amoss, P. "Cultural Centrality and Prestige for the Elderly: The Coast Salish
 Case." In *Dimensions: Aging, Culture, and Health,* edited by C. Frey.
 New York: Praeger, 1981.

Anderson, Ronald. "Political Clout of the Elderly to Grow in Coming
 Decades." *The Globe and Mail,* June 19, 1985.

Arling, Greg. "The Elderly Widow and Her Family, Neighbours and Friends."
 Journal of Marriage and the Family 38, no. 4 (1976): 757–768.

Armstrong, Pat, and Armstrong, Hugh. *A Working Majority. What Women
 Must Do For Pay.* Ottawa: Canadian Advisory Council on the Status
 of Women, 1983.

Aronson, Jane; Marshall, Victor W.; and Sulman, Joanne. "Patients Awaiting
 Discharge From Hospital." In *Aging in Canada. Social Perspectives,*
 2nd ed., edited by Victor W. Marshall, pp. 538–549. Don Mills,
 Ont.: Fitzhenry and Whiteside, 1987.

Ascah, Louis. "Recent Pension Reports in Canada: A Survey." *Canadian
 Public Policy* 10, no. 4 (1984): 415–428.

Atchley, Robert C. *Aging: Continuity and Change.* Belmont, California:
 Wadsworth, 1983.

———. "Selected Social and Psychological Differences Between Men and
 Women in Later Life." *Journal of Gerontology* 31, no. 2 (1976a):
 204–211.

———. *The Sociology of Retirement.* Cambridge, Mass.: Schenkman
 Publishing, 1976b.

Atkinson, T.H. *Trends in Life Satisfaction Among Canadians, 1968–1977.*
 Montreal: Institute for Research on Public Policy, 1979.

Auerbach, L., and Gerber, A. *Perceptions 2: Implications of the Changing Age
 Structure on the Canadian Population.* Ottawa: Science Council of
 Canada, 1976.

Babchuk, Nicholas. "Aging and Primary Relations." *International Journal of
 Aging and Human Development* 9, no. 2 (1978–79): 137–151.

Babin, Patrick. *Bias in Textbooks Regarding the Aged, Labour Unionists and
 Political Minorities.* Toronto: Ontario Ministry of Education, 1975.

Baillargeon, Richard. "Determinants of Early Retirement." *Canada's Mental Health* 30, no. 3 (1982): 20–22.

Baker, Maureen, ed. *The Family. Changing Trends in Canada.* Toronto: McGraw-Hill Ryerson, 1984.

———. *What Will Tomorrow Bring?* . . . *A Study of the Aspirations of Adolescent Women.* Ottawa: Canadian Advisory Council on the Status of Women, 1985.

Barnett, Rosalind C., and Baruch, Grace K. "Women in the Middle Years: A Critique of Research and Theory." *Psychology of Women Quarterly* 3, no. 2 (1978–79): 187–197.

Beaudoin, A., et al. "Non-Institutional Housing Conditions for the Aged." *Urban Renewal and Low-Income Housing* 9, no. 2 (1973): 14–22.

Beauvoir, Simone de. *Old Age.* Harmondsworth, England: Penguin Books, 1970.

Béland, François. "Living Arrangement Preferences among the Québec Elderly: Findings and Policy Implications." *Canadian Public Policy*, 12, no. a (1986).

Bengtson, Vern L. "Diversity and Symbolism in Grandparental Roles." In *Grandparenthood*, edited by Vern L. Bengtson and Joan F. Robertson, pp. 11–25. Beverly Hills: Sage, 1985.

Bernhardt, K.L., and Kinnear, T.C. "Profiling the Senior Citizen Market." *Proceedings of the Annual Convention of the Association for Consumer Research*, pp. 499–542. Chicago: Association for Consumer Research, 1977.

Bibby, Reginald. "Religionless Christianity: A Profile of Religion in the Canadian 80s." *Social Indicators Research* 13 (July, 1983): 1–16.

Binstock, R.H. "The Aged as Scapegoat." *The Gerontologist* 23 (1983): 136–143.

Blandford, Audrey. *Provincial Fact Book on Aging — Manitoba.* Prepared for 1st Manitoba Conference on Aging, May 21–24. Winnipeg: 1985.

Blau, Z.S. *Old Age in a Changing Society.* New York: Franklin Watts, 1973.

Branch, L.G., and Jette, A.M. "Elders' Use of Informal Long-Term Care Assistance." *The Gerontologist* 23 (1983): 51–56.

Brillon, Yves. *Victimization and Fear of Crime Among the Elderly.* Toronto: Butterworths, 1987.

Brown, Arnold S. "Satisfying Relationships for the Elderly and Their Patterns of Disengagement." *The Gerontologist* 12, no. 4 (1974): 363–367.

Bruhn, J. "An Ecological Perspective of Aging." *The Gerontologist* 11, no. 4 (1971): 318–321.

Brukaker, Timothy, ed. *Family Relationships in Later Life.* Beverly Hills: Sage, 1983.

Brunet, Jacques. "Care for the Elderly and Long Term Care in Canada and Quebec: Some Impacts of the National Direction." *Canadian Journal of Public Health* 76 (January/February 1985): 53–55.

Bryden, K. *Old Age Pensions and Policy-Making in Canada.* Montreal: McGill-Queen's University Press, 1974.

Burr, Wesley, R. "Satisfaction with Various Aspects of Marriage over the Life Cycle: A Random Middle-Class Sample." *Journal of Marriage and the Family* 32 (Feb. 1970).

Calvert, Geoffrey N. *Pensions and Survival. The Coming Crisis of Money and Retirement.* Toronto: Maclean-Hunter, 1977.

Canada, Government. *Better Pensions for Canadians.* Ottawa: Ministry of Supply and Services Canada, 1982.

Canada, House of Commons. *Report of the Parliamentary Task Force on Pension Reform.* Ottawa: Ministry of Supply and Services Canada, 1983.

Canada, Special Senate Committee on Retirement Age Policies. *Retirement Without Tears.* Ottawa: Canadian Government Publishing Centre, 1979.

Canadian Council on Social Development. *Beyond Shelter.* Ottawa: Canadian Council on Social Development, 1973.

Cantor, M. "Neighbours and Friends: An Overlooked Resource in the Informal Support System." *Research on Aging* 1 (1979): 434–463.

Cape, Elizabeth. "Aging Women in Rural Settings." In *Aging in Canada. Social Perspectives*, 2nd ed., edited by Victor W. Marshall, pp. 84–99. Don Mills, Ont.: Fitzhenry and Whiteside, 1987.

Carp, F. "Environmental Effects upon the Mobility of Older People." *Environment and Behaviour* 12, no. 2 (1980): 139–156.

Chappell, Neena, L. "Canadian Income and Health-Care Policy: Implications for the Elderly." In *Aging in Canada. Social Perspectives*, 2nd ed., edited by Victor W. Marshall, pp. 489–504. Don Mills, Ont.: Fitzhenry and Whiteside, 1987.

———. "The Future Impact of the Changing Status of Women." In *Canada's Changing Age Structure, Implications for the Future*, edited by Gloria M. Gutman. Burnaby, B.C.: Simon Fraser Publications, 1982.

———. "Informal Support Networks Among the Elderly." *Research on Aging* 5 (1983): 77–79.

———. "Social Policy and the Elderly." In *Aging in Canada. Social Perspectives*, edited by Victor W. Marshall, pp. 35–42. Don Mills, Ont.: Fitzhenry and Whiteside, 1980.

———. "Social Support and the Receipt of Home Care Services." *The Gerontologist* 25, no. 1 (1985): 47–54.

Chappell, Neena L., et al. *Aging and Health Care: A Social Perspective.* Toronto: Holt Rinehart & Winston, 1986.

Chappell, Neena L., and Havens, Betty. "Old and Female: Testing the Double Jeopardy Hypothesis." *The Sociological Quarterly* 21, no. 2 (1980): 157–171.

Chappell, Neena L., and Penning, M.J. "The Trend Away from Institutionalization, Humanism or Economic Efficiency." *Research on Aging* 1 (1979): 361–387.

Chen, Mervin Y.T. "Are Older Workers Marginal Workers?" Paper presented at the Annual Meetings of the Canadian Sociology and Anthropology Association, Montreal, 1985.

———. "Shaping Factors of Occupational Age Structures of the Female Labour Force in Canada." In *Aging in Canada. Social Perspectives*, 2nd ed., edited by Victor W. Marshall, pp. 158–175. Don Mills, Ont.: Fitzhenry and Whiteside, 1987.

Cicirelli, Victor G. "Relationship of Siblings to the Elderly Person's Feelings and Concerns." *Journal of Gerontology* 32, no. 3 (1977): 317–322.

Clarfield, A. Mark, and Paltiel, J.T. "The greying of China." *The Globe and Mail*, April 7, 1986, p. A7.

Clark, Phillip G. "The Social Allocation of Health Care Resources: Ethical Dilemmas in Age-group Competition." *The Gerontologist* 25, no. 2 (1985): 119–125.

Clark, R.L.; Maddox, G.L.; Schrimper, R.A.; and Sumner, D.A. *Inflation and the Economic Well-Being of the Elderly*. Baltimore: John Hopkins University Press, 1984.

Clark, R., and Spengler, J. "Changing Demography and Dependency Costs: The Implications of Future Dependency Ratios and their Composition." In *Aging and Income: Programs and Prospects of the Elderly*, edited by B. Herzog. New York: Human Services Press, 1978.

Clark, Susan, and Harvey, Andrew. "The Sexual Division of Labour: The Use of Time." *Atlantis* 2, no. 1 (1976): 46–66.

Connidis, Ingrid. "Life in Older Age: The View from the Top." In *Aging in Canada. Social Perspectives*, 2nd ed., edited by Victor W. Marshall, pp. 451–472. Don Mills, Ont.: Fitzhenry and Whiteside, 1987.

———. "The Service Needs of Older People: Implications for Public Policy." *Canadian Journal on Aging* 4, no. 1 (1985): 3–10.

———. "The Stigmatizing Effects of a Problem Orientation to Aging Research." *Canadian Journal of Social Work Education* 7, no. 2 (1981): 9–19.

———. "Women and Retirement: The Effect of Multiple Careers on Retirement Adjustment." *Canadian Journal on Aging* 1 (1982): 17–27.

Connidis, Ingrid, and Rempel, Judith. "The Living Arrangements of Older Residents: The Role of Gender, Marital Status, Age and Family Size." *Canadian Journal on Aging* 2, no. 3 (1983): 91–105.

Corin, Ellen. "The Relationship Between Formal and Informal Social Support Networks in Rural and Urban Contexts." In *Aging in Canada. Social Perspectives*, 2nd ed., edited by Victor W. Marshall, pp. 367–394. Don Mills, Ont.: Fitzhenry and Whiteside, 1987.

Costa, P., and McCrae, R. "Still Stable After All These Years: Personality as a Key to Some Issues in Aging." In *Life-Span Development and Behaviour*, edited by P. Baltes and O. Brim, vol. 3, pp. 65–102. New York: Academic Press, 1980.

Cowgill, D., and Holmes, L., eds. *Aging and Modernization*. New York: Appleton-Century-Crofts, 1972.

Crown, William H. "Some Thoughts on Reformulating the Dependency Ratio." *The Gerontologist* 25, no. 2 (1985): 166–171.

Cumming, E., et al. "Disengagement: A Tentative Theory of Aging." *Sociometry* 23, no. 1 (1960): 23–25.

Cumming, E., and Henry, W. *Growing Old: The Process of Disengagement*. New York: Basic Books, 1961.

Curtis, J.E., and White, P.G. "Age and Sport Participation: Decline in

Participation with Age or Increased Specialization with Age." In *Sport and the Sociological Imagination*, edited by N. Theberge and P. Donnelly, pp. 273–293. Fort Worth, Texas: Texas Christian University Press, 1984.

Cutler, Neil E. "Age Variations in the Dimensionality of Life Satisfaction." *Journal of Gerontology* 34, no. 4 (1979): 573–578.

Cutler, S. "Transportation and Changes in Life Satisfaction." *The Gerontologist* 15, no. 2 (1975): 155–159.

D'Arcy, Carl. "Aging and Mental Health." In *Aging in Canada. Social Perspectives*, 2nd ed., edited by Victor W. Marshall, pp. 424–450. Don Mills, Ont.: Fitzhenry and Whiteside, 1987.

Decker, David L. *Social Gerontology: An Introduction to the Dynamics of Aging*. Boston: Little, Brown & Co., 1980.

Delisle, Marc-André. "Elderly Peoples Management of Time and Leisure." *Canada's Mental Health*, September 1982, pp. 30–32.

Denton, Frank T.; Feaver, Christine H.; and Spencer, Byron G. "The Canadian Population and Labour Force: Retrospect and Prospect." In *Aging in Canada. Social Perspectives*, 2nd ed., edited by Victor W. Marshall, pp. 11–38. Don Mills, Ont.: Fitzhenry and Whiteside, 1987.

————. "Prospective Aging of the Population and Its Implications for the Labour Force and Government Expenditures." *Canadian Journal on Aging* 5, no. 2 (1986): 75–98.

Denton, Frank T.; Li, S. Neno; and Spencer, Byron G. "How Will Population Aging Affect the Future Costs of Maintaining Health-Care Standards." In *Aging in Canada: Social Perspectives*, 2nd ed., edited by Victor W. Marshall, pp. 553–568. Don Mills, Ont.: Fitzhenry and Whiteside, 1987.

Denton, Frank T., and Spencer, Byron G. "Population Aging and Future Health Costs in Canada." *Canadian Public Policy* 9, no. 2 (June 1983): 155–163.

Dowd, James J. "Aging as Exchange: A Preface to Theory." *Journal of Gerontology* 30 (1975): 584–594.

Drainie, Bronwyn. "Middle-age Spread on Campus." *The Globe and Mail*, April 3, 1986.

Driedger, Leo, and Chappell, Neena. *Aging and Ethnicity. Toward an Interface*. Toronto: Butterworths, 1987.

Driedger, Leo, and Mezoff, R.A. "Ethnic Prejudice and Discrimination in Winnipeg High Schools." *Canadian Journal of Sociology* 6, no. 1 (1981): 1–17.

Dulude, Louise. *Pension Reform With Women in Mind*. Ottawa: Canadian Advisory Council on the Status of Women, 1981.

————. *Women and Aging: A Report on the Rest of Our Lives*. Ottawa: Canadian Advisory Council on the Status of Women, 1978.

Elliott, Joyce. "The Daytime Television Drama Portrayal of Older Adults." *The Gerontologist* 24, no. 6 (1984): 628–633.

Epstein, S. "The Stability of Behaviour: 1. On Predicting Most of the People Much of the Time." *Journal of Personality and Social Psychology* 37, no. 7 (1979): 1097–1126.

Evans, Robert G. "Hang Together, or Hang Separately: The Viability of a Universal Health Care System in an Aging Society." *Canadian Public Policy* 13 (June 1987): 165–180.

———. *Strained Mercy: The Economics of Canadian Health Care.* Toronto: Butterworths, 1984.

Fengler, Alfred P. "Attitudinal Orientations of Wives Toward Their Husbands' Retirement." *International Journal of Aging and Human Development* 6, no. 2 (1975): 139–152.

Fengler, Alfred P., and Jensen, L. "Perceived and Objective Conditions as Predictors of the Life Satisfaction of Urban and Non-urban Elderly." *Journal of Gerontology* 36, no. 6 (1981): 750–752.

Fischer, David H. *Growing Old in America.* New York: Oxford University Press, 1977.

Foner, N. "Age and Social Change." In *Age and Anthropological Theory,* edited by D.I. Kertzer and J. Keith. Ithaca, N.Y.: Cornell University Press, 1984.

Foot, D. *Canada's Population Outlook. Demographic Futures and Economic Challenges.* Toronto: Lorimer, 1982.

Frideres, J.S. *Native People in Canada: Contemporary Conflicts.* Scarborough: Prentice-Hall Canada, 1983.

Fries, J.F. "The Compression of Morbidity: Miscellaneous Comments About a Theme." *The Gerontologist* 4 (1984): 354–359.

Gaffield, Chad. "Wage Labour, Industrialization, and the Origins of the Modern Family." In *The Family. Changing Trends in Canada,* edited by Maureen Baker, pp. 21–34. Toronto: McGraw-Hill Ryerson, 1984.

Gantz, W., et al. "Approaching Invisibility: The Portrayal of the Elderly in Magazine Advertising." *Journal of Communications* 30, no. 1 (1980): 56–60.

Gee, Ellen M. "Historical Change in the Family Life Course of Canadian Men and Women." In *Aging in Canada. Social Perspectives,* 2nd ed., edited by Victor W. Marshall, pp. 265–287. Don Mills, Ont.: Fitzhenry and Whiteside, 1987.

Gee, Ellen M., and Kimball, Meredith M. *Women and Aging.* Toronto: Butterworths, 1987.

Gelb, B.D. "Exploring the Gray Market Segment." *MSU Business Topics* 26 (1978): 41–46.

George, Linda K.; Mutran, Elizabeth J.; and Pennybacker, Margaret R. "The Meaning and Measurement of Age Identity." *Experimental Aging Research* 6, no. 3 (1980): 283–298.

Gerbner, G., et al. "Aging with Television: Images on Television Drama and Conceptions of Social Reality." *Journal of Communications* 30, no. 1 (1980): 37–47.

Gifford, C.G. "Grey is Strong." *Policy Options,* October 1985, pp. 16–18.

Gold Delores. "Sex Differences in the Experience of Aging." *Canadian Woman Studies* 5, no. 3 (Spring 1984): 32–34.

Goudy, Willis J., and Goudreau Jr., John F. "Social Ties and Life Satisfaction of Older Persons: Another Evaluation." *Journal of Gerontological Social Work* 4, no. 1 (1981): 35–50.

Graebner, William. *A History of Retirement.* New Haven, Conn.: Yale University Press, 1980.

Graney, M., and Zimmerman, R. "Health Self-Report Correlates Among Older People in National Random Sample Data." *Mid-American Review of Sociology* 5, no. 2 (1980): 47–59.

Green, Susan. "Attitudes and Perceptions About the Elderly: Current and Future Perspectives." *International Journal of Aging and Human Development* 13, no. 2 (1981): 99–119.

Gross, M. John, and Schwenger, Cope W. *Health Care Costs for the Elderly in Ontario: 1976–2026.* Toronto: Ontario Economic Council, 1981.

Gruenberg, E.M. "The Failure of Success." *Milbank Memorial Fund Quarterly/Health and Society* 55 (1977): 3–24.

Gubrium, J. *The Myth of the Golden Years: A Socio-Environmental Theory of Aging.* Springfield, Illinois: Charles C. Thomas, 1973.

Guillemard, Anne-Marie, ed. *Old Age and the Welfare State.* Beverly Hills: Sage, 1983.

Gutman, Gloria M., ed. *Canada's Changing Age Structure, Implications for the Future.* Burnaby, B.C.: Simon Fraser Publications, 1982.

————. "The Elderly at Home and in Retirement Housing: A Comparative Study of Health Problems, Functional Difficulties, and Support Service." In *Aging in Canada. Social Perspectives,* edited by Victor W. Marshall, pp. 189–200. Don Mills, Ont.: Fitzhenry and Whiteside, 1980.

Haber, Carole. "Mandatory Retirement in Nineteenth-Century America: The Conceptual Basis for a New Work Cycle." *Journal of Social History* 12 (1978): 77–96.

Hall, M. Ann, and Richardson, Dorothy A. *Fair Ball. Towards Sex Equality in Canadian Sport.* Ottawa: Canadian Advisory Council on the Status of Women in Canada, 1983.

Harris, Louis, et al. *The Myth and Reality of Aging in America.* Washington, D.C.: National Council on Aging, 1975.

Harvey, Carol D. and Bahr, Howard M. *The Sunshine Widows.* Lexington, Mass.: Lexington Books, 1980.

Hauser, P.M. "Aging and World-wide Population Change." In *Handbook of Aging and the Social Sciences,* edited by B.H. Binstock and E. Shanas. New York: Van Nostrand Reinhold Co., 1976.

Havens, Betty, and Chappell, Neena L. "Triple Jeopardy: Age, Sex and Ethnicity." *Canadian Ethnic Studies* 15, no. 3 (1983): 113–131.

Havighurst, Robert J., et al. "Disengagement and Patterns of Aging." In *Middle Age and Aging,* edited by B. Neugarten. Chicago: University of Chicago Press, 1968.

Health and Welfare Canada. *Basic Facts on Social Security Programs.* Ottawa: Health and Welfare Canada, 1985.

————. *Canadian Governmental Report on Aging.* Ottawa: Health and Welfare Canada, 1982.

————. *Fact Book on Aging in Canada.* Ottawa: Health and Welfare Canada, 1983.

————. *Manitoba/Canada Home Care Study: An Overview of the Results.* Ottawa: Policy, Planning, and Information Branch, 1982.

———. *Profiles on Home Care/Home Support Programs*. Ottawa: Health and Welfare Canada, 1982.

Heller, Peter S.; Hemming, Richard; Kohnert, Peter W.; et al. *Aging and Social Expenditure in the Major Industrial Countries, 1980–2025*. Washington, D.C.: International Monetary Fund, 1986.

Hendricks, Jon, and Hendricks, C. Davis. *Aging in Mass Society: Myths and Realities*. Cambridge, Mass.: Winthrop Publishers, 1977.

Hess, Beth B., and Markson, Elizabeth W. *Aging and Old Age*. New York: Macmillan Publishing, 1980.

———. *Growing Old in America. New Perspectives on Aging*. 3rd ed. New Brunswick, N.J.: Transaction, 1985.

Hill, Elizabeth A., and Dorfman, Lorraine T. "Reaction of Housewives to the Retirement of Their Husbands." *Family Relations* 31 (1982): 195–200.

Hirdes, John P.; Brown, K. Stephen; and Forbes, William F. "The Association Between Self-Reported Income and Perceived Health Based on the Ontario Longitudinal Study of Aging." *Canadian Journal on Aging* 5, no. 3 (1986): 189–204.

Hodge, G.D., and Qadeer, M.A. *Towns and Villages in Canada: The Importance of Being Unimportant*. Toronto: Butterworths, 1983.

Holmberg, A. *Nomads of a Long Bow*. Garden City, N.Y.: Natural History Press, 1969.

Holtzman, Joseph M., and Hiroko, Akiyama. "What Children See: The Aged on Television in Japan and the United States." *The Gerontologist* 25, no. 1 (1985): 62–68.

Horlick, Max, and Skolnik, Alfred M. *Mandating Private Pensions: A Study on European Experience*. Washington: Department of Health, Education and Welfare, 1978.

Hulicka, Irene, et al. "Perceived Latitude of Choice of Institutionalized and Non-Institutionalized Elderly Women." *Experimental Aging Research* 1 (1975): 27–39.

Hutchinson, Allan, and Petter, Andrew. "Many Pay for Privilege of Few." *Perception* 9, no. 2 (1986): 17–18.

James, Timothy, M. "The Trade." *The Wilson Quarterly* 9, no. 1 (1985): 107–125.

Johnston, Richard. "Political Generations and Electoral Mobilization in Canada." Paper prepared for Conference on Generations and Political Change, Laval University, Quebec, June 19–20, 1986.

Kalbach, Warren, and McVey, Wayne. *The Demographic Bases of Canadian Society*. 2nd ed. Toronto: McGraw-Hill Ryerson, 1979.

Kaye, Lenard W. "Home Care for the Aged: A Fragile Partnership." *Social Work* 30, no. 4 (July-August, 1985): 312–317.

Kernaghan K., and Kuper, O. *Coordinating in Canadian Governments: A Case Study of Aging Policy*. Toronto: Institute of Public Administration, 1983.

Kettle, John. *The Big Generation*. Toronto: McClelland & Stewart, 1980.

Kimmel, Douglas C.; Price, Karl P.; and Walker, James W. "Retirement Choice and Retirement Satisfaction." *Journal of Gerontology* 33, no. 4 (1978): 575–585.

Klemmack, David L., and Roff, Lucinda Lee. "Fear of Personal Aging and Subjective Well-Being in Later Life." *Journal of Gerontology* 39, no. 6 (1984): 756–758.

Kline, Chrysee. "The Socialization Process of Women: Implications for a Theory of Successful Aging." *Gerontologist* 15, no. 6 (1975): 486–492.

Kohn, J., and Kohn, W. *The Widower*. Boston: Beacon Press, 1979.

Koninck, Maria de. "Double Work and Women's Health." *Canada's Mental Health*, September 1985, pp. 28–31.

Koyl, L.F. "The Aging Canadian." In *Canadian Gerontological Collection I*, edited by B.T. Wigdor, pp. 57–79, Toronto: Canadian Association on Gerontology, 1977.

Kramer, M. "The Increasing Prevalence of Mental Disorders: Implications for the Future." Paper presented at National Conference on the Elderly Deinstitutionalized Patient in the Community, Arlington, Virginia, May 28, 1981.

Kraus, Arthur S. "The Burden of Care for Families of Elderly Persons with Dementia." *Canadian Journal on Aging* 3, no. 1 (1984): 45–51.

———. "The Increase in the Usual Life Span in North America." *Canadian Journal on Aging* 6, no. 1 (1987): 19–31.

Krehm, William. "Prepare for the Pensioner Boom." *Policy Options*, July 1985, pp. 16–18.

Kuhn, Maggie. "Challenge to a New Age." In *Readings in the Political Economy of Aging*, edited by Meredith Minkler and Carroll L. Estes. Farmingdale, New York: Baywood Publishing Co., 1984.

Lapierre, Louise. *Canadian Women: Profile of Their Health*. Ottawa: Statistics Canada, 1984.

Larson, Reed. "Thirty Years of Research on the Subjective Well-Being of Older Americans." *Journal of Gerontology* 33, no. 1 (1978): 109–125.

Laslett, Peter. *The World We Have Lost*. London: University Paperbacks, 1971.

Lee, G., and Lassey, M. "Rural-Urban Differences Among the Elderly: Economic, Social and Subjective Factors." *Journal of Social Issues* 36, no. 2 (1980): 62–74.

Lee, John Alan. "The Invisible Lives of Canada's Gray Gays." In *Aging in Canada. Social Perspectives*, 2nd ed., edited by Victor W. Marshall, pp. 138–155. Don Mills, Ont.: Fitzhenry and Whiteside, 1987.

Lehr, Ursula. "The Situation of Elderly Women: Psychological and Social Aspects." *Zeitschrift für Gerontologie* 11, no. 1 (1978): 6–26. Abstracted in *Psychological Abstracts* 61:1356.

Levinson, Daniel J., et al. *The Seasons of a Man's Life*. New York: Ballantine, 1978.

Li, Peter S. "The Use of Oral History in Studying Elderly Chinese-Canadians." *Canadian Ethnic Studies* 17, no. 1 (1985): 67–77.

List, Wilfred. "Should Forced Retirement be Banned?" *The Globe and Mail*, May 27, 1985.

Longino, C.F., and Biggar, J.C. "The Impact of Retirement Migration on the South." *The Gerontologist* 21 (1981): 283–290.

Lopata, Helena. "The Social Involvement of American Widows." *American Behavioural Scientist* 14, no. 1 (1970): 40–56.

———. *Widowhood in an American City*. Cambridge, Mass.: Schenkman Publishing Co., 1973.

———. *Women as Widows: Support Systems*. New York: Elseviers, 1979.

Lowenthal, M., and Robinson, B. "Social Networks and Isolation." In *Handbook of Aging and the Social Sciences*, edited by R. Binstock and E. Shanas. New York: Van Nostrand Reinhold, 1976.

Lumpkin, James R. "The Effect of Retirement Versus Age on the Shopping Orientations of the Older Consumer." *The Gerontologist* 24, no. 6 (1984): 622–627.

Lupri, Eugen, and Frideres, James. "The Quality of Marriage and the Passage of Time: Marital Satisfaction Over the Family Life Cycle." *The Canadian Journal of Sociology* 6 (1981): 283–306.

Luxton, Meg. *More Than a Labour of Love*. Toronto: Women's Press, 1980.

Manton, K.G. "Changing Concepts of Mortality and Morbidity in the Elderly Population." *Milbank Memorial Fund Quarterly* 60 (1982): 183–244.

Marcus, L. "The Old and Their Families: Myths and Realities." Paper presented to the National Symposium on Aging, Ottawa, October 1978.

Marshall, Victor W., ed. *Aging in Canada. Social Perspectives*. Don Mills, Ont.: Fitzhenry and Whiteside, 1980.

———. *Aging in Canada. Social Perspectives*. 2nd ed. Don Mills, Ont.: Fitzhenry and Whiteside, 1987.

———. "Generations, Age Groups and Cohorts: Conceptual Distinctions." *Canadian Journal of Aging* 2, no. 2 (1983): 51–62.

———. "Social Characteristics of Future Aged." In *Housing for an Aging Population: Alternatives*, edited by B.T. Wigdor and Louise Ford. Toronto: University of Toronto, Program in Gerontology, 1981.

———. "Socialization for Impending Death in a Retirement Village." *American Journal of Sociology* 80 (1975): 1124–1144.

Martin, J. David. "Power Dependence, and the Complaints of the Elderly: A Social Exchange Perspective." *Aging and Human Development* 2 (1971): 108–112.

Martin, James K. "Social Policy Concerns Related to Retirement: Implications for Research." In *Canada's Changing Age Structure, Implications for Social Research*, edited by Gloria M. Gutman. Burnaby, B.C.: Simon Fraser University Publications, 1982.

Mason, J.B., and Bearden, W.O. "Elderly Shopping Behaviour and Marketplace Perceptions." *Proceedings of the Annual Convention of the Southern Marketing Association*, pp. 290–293. New Orleans: Southern Marketing Association, 1978.

Matthews, Anne Martin. "Widowhood as an Expectable Life Event." In *Aging in Canada. Social Perspectives*, 2nd ed., edited by Victor W. Marshall, pp. 343–366. Don Mills, Ont.: Fitzhenry and Whiteside, 1987.

———. "Women and Widowhood." In *Aging in Canada. Social Perspectives*, edited by Victor W. Marshall, pp. 145–153. Don Mills, Ont.: Fitzhenry and Whiteside, 1980.

Maxwell, R., and Silverman, P. "Information and Esteem: Cultural Considerations in the Treatment of the Aged." *Aging and Human Development* 1, no. 4 (1970): 361–392.

McClain, Jan, ed. *Housing the Elderly.* Ottawa: Canadian Council on Social Development, 1976.

McCrae, Robert R., and Costa Jr., Paul T. *Emerging Lives, Enduring Dispositions: Personality in Adulthood.* Boston: Little, Brown & Co., 1984.

McDaniel, Susan A., *Canada's Aging Population.* Toronto: Butterworths, 1986.

———. "Shifting Opportunities in Canada's Aging Society: Contrasting Prospects for Men and for Women." Paper presented at the Annual Meetings of the Canadian Sociology and Anthropology Association, Montreal, 1985.

McDonald, P. Lynn, and Wanner, Richard A. "Retirement in a Dual Economy." In *Aging in Canada. Social Perspectives*, 2nd ed., edited by Victor W. Marshall, pp. 245–264. Don Mills, Ont.: Fitzhenry and Whiteside, 1987.

———. "Socioeconomic Determinants of Early Retirement in Canada." *Canadian Journal on Aging* 3, no. 3 (1984): 105–116.

McKenzie, Helen. "Health Care Costs: Policies and Legislation in Four OECD Nations." Ottawa: Library of Parliament, Research Branch, 1985.

McKenzie, Helen, and Stilborn, Jack. "Social Benefits for Senior Citizens: An International Comparison." Ottawa: Library of Parliament, Research Branch, 1985.

McKim, William A., and Mishara, Brian L. *Drugs and Aging.* Toronto: Butterworths, 1987.

McPherson, Barry D. *Aging as a Social Process.* Toronto: Butterworths, 1983.

McPherson, Barry D., and Kozlik, Carol A. "Age Patterns in Leisure Participation: The Canadian Case." In *Aging in Canada. Social Perspectives*, 2nd ed., edited by Victor W. Marshall, pp. 211–227. Don Mills, Ont.: Fitzhenry and Whiteside, 1987.

Meissner, Martin; Humphreys, Elizabeth; Meis, Scott; and Scheu, William. "No Exit for Wives: Sexual Division of Labour and the Cumulation of Household Demands." *Canadian Review of Sociology and Anthropology* 12 — part 1 (1975): 424–439.

Messinger, Hans, and Powell, Brian J. "The Implications of Canada's Aging Society on Social Expenditures." In *Aging in Canada. Social Perspectives*, 2nd ed., edited by Victor W. Marshall, pp. 569–585. Don Mills, Ont.: Fitzhenry and Whiteside, 1987.

Morgan, L. "A Reexamination of Widowhood and Morale." *Journal of Gerontology* 31, no. 6 (1976): 687–695.

Morton, Mildred J. "Pensions and Women." Ottawa: Library of Parliament, Research Branch, 1984.

Moseley, Charles J. "Who Cares for the Elderly?" *Editorial Research Reports* 11, no. 19 (1986): 855–871.

Myers, Anita M., and Gonda, Gail. "Research on Physical Activity in the Elderly: Practical Implications for Program Planning." *Canadian Journal on Aging* 5, no. 3 (1986): 175–187.

Myles, John F. "Comparative Public Policies for the Elderly: Frameworks and Resources for Analysis." In *Old Age and the Welfare State*, edited by Anne-Marie Guillemard, pp. 19–44. Beverly Hills: Sage, 1983.

———. "Institutionalization and Disengagement among the Elderly." *Canadian Review of Sociology and Anthropology* 16 (1979): 171–182.

———. *Old Age and the Welfare State. The Political Economy of Public Pensions.* Toronto: Little, Brown & Co., 1984.

Myles, John F., and Boyd, Monica. "Population Aging and the Elderly." In *Social Issues, Sociological Views of Canada*, edited by D. Forcese and S. Richer. Scarborough, Ont.: Prentice-Hall, 1982.

National Council of Welfare. *Better Pensions for Homemakers.* Ottawa: National Council of Welfare, May 1984a.

———. *Sixty-Five and Older.* Ottawa: National Council of Welfare, February 1984b.

Nett, Emily. "The Family and Aging." In *The Family. Changing Trends in Canada*, edited by Maureen Baker, pp. 129–161. Toronto: McGraw-Hill Ryerson, 1984.

Neugarten, B. "The Middle Generations." In *Aging Parents*, edited by P. Ragan, pp. 258–266. Los Angeles: University of Southern California Press, 1979.

Neugarten, Bernice L.; Havighurst, Robert; and Tobin, Sheldon S. "Personality and Patterns of Aging." In *Middle Age and Aging*, edited by B. Neugarten, pp. 173–177. Chicago: Chicago University Press, 1968.

Neysmith, Sheila M. "Marginality and Morale." In *Aging in Canada, Social Perspectives*, edited by Victor W. Marshall, pp. 281–285. Don Mills, Ont.: Fitzhenry and Whiteside, 1980.

———. "Social Policy Implications of an Aging Society." In *Aging in Canada. Social Perspectives*, 2nd ed., edited by Victor W. Marshall, pp. 586–597. Don Mills, Ont.: Fitzhenry and Whiteside, 1987.

Neysmith, Sheila, and Edwardh, Joey. "Economic Dependency in the 1980s: Its Impact on Third World Elderly." *Aging and Society* 4, no. 1 (1984): 21–44.

———. "Ideological Underpinnings of the World Assembly on Aging." *Canadian Journal on Aging* 2, no. 3 (1983): 125–136.

Nicholson, John: *Seven Ages.* Glasglow: Fontana Paperbacks, 1980.

Nishio, Harry K., and Lank, Heather. "Patterns of Labour Participation of Older Female Workers." In *Aging in Canada. Social Perspectives*, 2nd ed., edited by Victor W. Marshall, pp. 228–244. Don Mills, Ont.: Fitzhenry and Whiteside, 1987.

Norris, Joan E. "Psychological Processes in the Development of Later-Life Social Identity." In *Aging in Canada. Social Perspectives*, 2nd ed., edited by Victor W. Marshall, pp. 60–81. Don Mills, Ont.: Fitzhenry and Whiteside, 1987.

Northcott, Herbert C. "The Best Years of Your Life." *Canadian Journal on Aging* 1, no. 3 (1982): 72–78.

———. "The Interprovincial Migration of Canada's Elderly: 1956–61 and 1971–76." *Canadian Journal on Aging* 3, no. 1 (1984): 3–21.

Novak, Mark. *Successful Aging, The Myths, Realities and Future of Aging in Canada.* Markham, Ont.: Penguin, 1985.

Nydegger, C. "Family Ties of the Aged in Cross-Cultural Perspective." *The Gerontologist* 23 (1983): 26–32.

Organization for Economic Co-operation and Development. *Public Expenditure on Income Maintenance Programmes.* Paris: OECD, 1976.

Palmore, Erdman. "Attitudes Toward the Aged: What We Know and What We Need to Know." *Research on Aging* 4, no. 3 (1982): 333–348.

———. *The Honourable Elders: A Cross Cultural Analysis of Aging in Japan.* Durham, North Carolina: Duke University Press, 1975.

Palmore, Erdman; Cleveland, William P.; Nowlin, John B.; Ramm, Dietolf; and Siegler, Ilene. "Stress and Adaptation in Later Life." *Journal of Gerontology* 34, no. 6 (1979): 841–851.

Palmore, Erdman, and Manton, K. "Modernization and the Status of the Aged: International Correlations." *Journal of Gerontology* 29, no. 2 (1974): 205–210.

Pampel, Fred C., and Park, Sookja. "Cross-national Patterns and Determinants of Female Retirement." *American Journal of Sociology* 91, no. 4 (1986): 932–955.

Pampel, Fred C., and Weiss, Jane. "Economic Development, Pension Policies, and the Labour Force Participation of Aged Males: A Cross-National, Longitudinal Study." *American Journal of Sociology* 89 (September 1983): 350–372.

Parker, Stanley. *Work and Retirement.* London: Allen and Unwin, 1982.

Plath, D. "Japan: The After Years." In *Aging and Modernization,* edited by D. Cowgill and L. Holmes. New York: Appleton-Century-Crofts, 1972.

Posner, Judith. "Old and Female: The Double Whammy." In *Aging in Canada. Social Perspectives,* edited by Victor W. Marshall, pp. 80–87. Don Mills, Ont.: Fitzhenry and Whiteside, 1980.

Powell, Lawrence A., and Williamson, John B. "The Mass Media and the Aged." *Social Policy* 16 — Summer (1985): 38–49.

Pratt, Henry J. "Aging Policy and Process In Canadian Federal Government." *Canadian Public Administration* 30, no. 1 (1987): 57–75.

Quinn, Joseph F. "Job Characteristics and Early Retirement." *Industrial Relations* 17, no. 3 (1978): 315–323.

Reed, Christopher. "Despite No-Fault, Wives Lose." *The Globe and Mail,* February 11, 1986.

Regush, Nicholas. "Life Expectancy for Montreal's Poor Nine Years Shorter than for Rich: Study." *Ottawa Citizen,* January 31, 1987.

Reid, David W., and Ziegler, Michael. "A Survey of the Reinforcements and Activities Elderly Citizens Feel Are Important for Their General Happiness." *Essence* 2, no. 1 (1977): 5–24.

Reinharz, Shulamit. "Friends or Foes: Gerontological and Feminist Theory." *Women's Studies International Forum* 9, no. 5 (1986): 503–514.

Rhoads, E.C. "Reevaluation of the Aging and Modernization Theory: The Samoan Evidence." *The Gerontologist* 24 (1984): 243–250.

Rice, D.P., and Feldman, J.J. "Living Longer in the United States: Demographic Changes and Health Needs for the Elderly." *Milbank Memorial Fund Quarterly* 61 (1983): 430–444.

Riley, Matilda W., and Foner, Anne. *Aging and Society, Vol. 2: Aging and the Professions.* New York: Russell Sage Foundation, 1968.

Roadburg, Alan. *Aging, Retirement, Leisure and Work in Canada.* Toronto: Methuen, 1985.

Rollins, Boyd C., and Feldman, Harold. "Marital Satisfaction over the Family Life Cycle." *Journal of Marriage and the Family* 32 (1970): 20–28.

Rose, Arnold M. "The Subculture of Aging: A Framework for Research in Social Gerontology." In *Older People and Their Social World*, edited by A.M. Rose and W.A. Peterson, pp. 3–16. Philadelphia: F.A. Davis Co., 1965.

Rosenthal, Carolyn J. "Aging and Intergenerational Relations in Canada." In *Aging in Canada. Social Perspectives*, 2nd ed., edited by Victor W. Marshall, pp. 311–342. Don Mills, Ont.: Fitzhenry and Whiteside, 1987.

———. "The Differentiation of Multigenerational Households." *Canadian Journal on Aging* 5, no. 1, (1986).

Rundall, T.G., and Evashwick, C. "Social Networks and Help-Seeking Among the Elderly." Paper presented at the 33rd Annual Scientific Meeting of the Gerontological Society, San Diego, California, November 1980.

Schlesinger, Rachel Aber. "Granny-Bashing: An Introduction to the Problem." *Canadian Woman Studies* 5, no. 3, (1984): 56–59.

Schmitt, Neal, et al. "Comparison of Early Retirees and Non-Retirees." *Personnel Psychology* 32 (1979): 327–340.

Schneider, E.L., and Brody, J.A. "Aging, Natural Death and the Compression of Morbidity: Another View." *New England Journal of Medicine*, October 6, 1983, pp. 854–856.

Schrimper, Ronald A., and Clark, Robert L. "Health Expenditures and Elderly Adults." *Journal of Gerontology* 40, no. 2 (1985): 235–243.

Schwenger, Cope W. "Formal Health Care for the Elderly in Canada." In *Aging in Canada. Social Perspectives*, 2nd ed., edited by Victor W. Marshall, pp. 505–519. Don Mills, Ont.: Fitzhenry and Whiteside, 1987.

Scott, Jean P. "Siblings and Other Kin." In *Family Relationships in Later Life*, edited by Timothy Brukaker. Beverly Hills: Sage, 1983.

Seleen, Diane R. "The Congruence Between the Actual and Desired Use of Time by Older Adults: A Predictor of Life Satisfaction." *The Gerontologist* 22, no. 1 (1982): 95–99.

Shanas, Ethel. "The Family as a Social Support System in Old Age." *The Gerontologist* 19, no. 2 (1979): 169–174.

———. "Older People and Their Families: The New Pioneers." *Journal of Marriage and the Family* 42, no. 1 (1980): 9–15.

Shanas, Ethel, et al. *Older People in Three Industrial Societies.* New York: Atherton Press, 1967.

Shapiro, Evelyn, and Roos, N.P. "High Users of Hospital Days." *Canadian Journal on Aging* 5, no. 3 (1986): 165–174.

———. "Predictors, Patterns and Consequences of Nursing-Home Use in One Canadian Province." In *Aging in Canada. Social Perspectives*, 2nd ed., edited by Victor W. Marshall, pp. 520–537. Don Mills, Ont.: Fitzhenry and Whiteside, 1987.

Sheehy, Gail. *Passages: Predictable Crises in Adult Life.* New York: Dutton, 1974.

Shephard, Roy J. "Critical Issues in the Health of the Elderly: The Role of Physical Activity." *Canadian Journal on Aging* 3, no. 4 (1984): 199–208.

Sherman, S.R. "Mutual Assistance and Support in Retirement Housing." *Journal of Gerontology* 30 (1975): 479–483.

Shkop, Yitzchak M. "The Impact of Job Modification Options of Retirement Plans." *Industrial Relations* 21, no. 2 (1982): 261–267.

Shulman, N. "The Aging of Urban Canada." In *Aging in Canada. Social Perspectives*, edited by Victor W. Marshall, pp. 27–34. Don Mills, Ont.: Fitzhenry and Whiteside, 1980.

Simmons-Tropea, Daryl, and Osborn, Richard. "Disease, Survival and Death: The Health Status of Canada's Elderly." In *Aging in Canada. Social Perspectives*, 2nd ed., edited by Victor W. Marshall, pp. 399–423. Don Mills, Ont.: Fitzhenry and Whiteside, 1987.

Skogland, John. "Job Deprivation in Retirement: Anticipated and Experienced Feelings." *Research on Aging* 1, no. 4 (1979): 481–493.

Smith E., and Serfass, R., eds. *Exercise and Aging: The Scientific Process.* Hillside, N.J.: Enslow Publishers, 1981.

Smith, Kenneth J., and Lipman, Aaron. "Constraint and Life Satisfaction." *Journal of Gerontology* 27, no. 1 (1972): 77–82.

Snider, Earle L. "Explaining Life Satisfaction: It's the Elderly Attitudes That Count." *Social Science Quarterly* 61, no. 2 (1980): 253–263.

Statistics Canada. *Births and Deaths 1985.* Cat. 84–204. Ottawa: Ministry of Supply and Services, November 1986.

———. *Culture Statistics Recreational Activities 1976.* Cat. 87–501. Ottawa: Ministry of Supply and Services, November 1978.

———. *Education in Canada: A Statistical Review for 1982–83.* Cat. 81–229. Ottawa: Ministry of Supply and Services, June 1984.

———. *The Elderly in Canada.* Cat. 99–932. Ottawa: Ministry of Supply and Services, April 1984.

———. *Income Distributions By Size in Canada,* (Preliminary Estimates, 1985). Cat. 13–206. Ottawa: Ministry of Supply and Services, September 1986.

———. *The Labour Force.* Cat. 71–001. Ottawa: Ministry of Supply and Services, January 1986.

———. *The Labour Force.* Cat. 71–001. Ottawa: Ministry of Supply and Services, January 1987.

———. *Pension Plans in Canada, 1984.* Cat. 74–401. Ottawa: Ministry of Supply and Services, August 1986.

———. *Perspectives Canada III.* Cat. 11–511. Ottawa: Ministry of Supply and Services, April 1980.

————. *Population Projections for Canada, Provinces and Territories 1984–2006*. Cat. 91–520. Ottawa: Ministry of Supply and Services, May 1985.

————. *Women in Canada, A Statistical Report*. Cat. 89–503. Ottawa: Ministry of Supply and Services, March 1985.

Stephens, Thomas; Craig, Cora L.; and Ferris, Blake F. "Adult Physical Activity in Canada: Findings from the Canadian Fitness Survey I." *Canadian Journal of Public Health* 77 (1986): 285–290.

Stolar, G. Elaine; Hill, Mary A.; and Tomblin, Alanna. "Family Disengagement — Myth or Reality: A Follow-up Study After Geriatric Assessment." *Canadian Journal on Aging* 5, no. 2 (1986): 113–123.

Stone, Leroy O., and Fletcher, Susan. *A Profile of Canada's Older Population*. Montreal: Institute for Research on Public Policy, 1980.

————. "The Hypothesis of Age Patterns in Living Arrangement Passages." In *Aging in Canada. Social Perspectives*, 2nd ed., edited by Victor W. Marshall, pp. 288–310. Don Mills, Ont.: Fitzhenry and Whiteside, 1987.

Storm, Christine; Storm, Thomas; and Strike-Schurman, Janet. "Obligations for Care: Beliefs in a Small Canadian Town." *Canadian Journal on Aging* 4, no. 2 (1985): 75–85.

Strain, L., and Chappell, Neena, L. "Confidants: Do They Make a Difference in Quality of Life." *Research on Aging* 4 (1982): 479–502.

Streib, Gordon F., and Schneider, Clement J. *Retirement in American Society*. Ithaca, N.Y.: Cornell University Press, 1972.

Stryckman, Judith. "Work Sharing and the Older Worker in a Unionized Setting." In *Aging in Canada. Social Perspectives*, 2nd ed., edited by Victor W. Marshall, pp. 193–208. Don Mills, Ont.: Fitzhenry and Whiteside, 1987.

Synge, Jane. "Work and Family Support Patterns of the Aged in the Early Twentieth Century." In *Aging in Canada. Social Perspectives*, edited by Victor W. Marshall, pp. 135–144. Don Mills, Ont.: Fitzhenry and Whiteside, 1980.

Synge, Jane, et al. "Phoning and Writing as Means of Keeping in Touch in the Family of Later Life." Paper presented at Annual Meetings of Canadian Association on Gerontology, Toronto, November 1981.

Taylor, Malcolm. *Health Insurance and Canadian Public Policy*. Montreal: McGill-Queen's University Press, 1978.

Thoits, P. "Conceptual, Methodological and Theoretical Problems in Studying Social Support as A Buffer Against Life Stress." *Journal of Health and Social Behavior* 23 (1982): 145–159.

Thomae, H., ed. *Patterns of Aging: Findings from the Bonn Longitudinal Study of Aging*. New York: S. Karger, 1976.

Thompson, Enid. "Aging in Manitoba." In *Housing the Elderly*, edited by Jan McClain, pp. 32–37. Ottawa: Council on Social Development, 1978.

Thurnher, Majda. "Goals, Values and Life Evaluations at the Preretirement Stage." *Journal of Gerontology* 29, no. 1 (1974): 85–96.

Tindale, Joseph A., "Age, Seniority and Class Patterns of Job Strain." In *Aging in Canada. Social Perspectives*, 2nd ed., edited by Victor W.

Marshall, pp. 176–192. Don Mills, Ont.: Fitzhenry and Whiteside, 1987.

Tindale, Joseph A., and Marshall, Victor W. "A Generational-Conflict Perspective for Gerontology." In *Aging in Canada. Social Perspectives*, edited by Victor W. Marshall, pp. 43–50. Don Mills, Ont.: Fitzhenry and Whiteside, 1980.

Towle, J.G., and Martin Jr., C.R. "The Elderly Consumer: One Segment or Many?" *Proceedings of the Annual Convention of the Association for Consumer Research*, pp. 463–468. San Francisco: Association for Consumer Research, 1975.

Troll, L. "The Family of Later Life: A Decade Review." *Journal of Marriage and the Family* 33, no. 2 (1971): 263–290.

Troll, L., and Parron, E. "Age Changes in Sex Roles Amid Changing Sex Roles: The Double Shift." In *Annual Review of Gerontology and Geriatrics*, Vol. 2, pp. 118–143. New York: Springer Publishing Company, 1981.

Ujimoto, K. Victor. "The Ethnic Dimensions of Aging in Canada." In *Aging in Canada. Social Perspectives*, 2nd ed., edited by Victor W. Marshall, pp. 111–137. Don Mills, Ont.: Fitzhenry and Whiteside, 1987.

United Nations. *The World Aging Situation: Strategies and Policies*. New York: United Nations, 1985.

———. *World Statistics in Brief*. New York: United Nations, 1983.

United States Congress. *Technology and Aging in America*. Washington: Office of Technology Assessment, 1985.

United States Department of Health and Human Services. *Social Security Programs Throughout the World — 1983*. Research Report No. 59. Washington: U.S. Government Printing Office, 1984.

Vachon, Mary L.S. "Grief and Bereavement Following the Death of a Spouse." *Canadian Psychiatric Association Journal* 21, no. 1 (1976): 35–44.

———. "Identity Change Over the First Two Years of Bereavement: Social Relationships and Social Support." Ph.D. dissertation, York University, 1979.

Vanderburgh, Rosamond M. "Modernization and Aging in the Anicinabe Context." In *Aging in Canada. Social Perspectives*, 2nd ed., edited by Victor W. Marshall, pp. 100–110. Don Mills, Ont.: Fitzhenry and Whiteside, 1987.

Veevers, Jean. *Childless by Choice*. Toronto: Butterworths, 1980.

Verzuh, Ron. "Grey Power Comes Out of the Closet." *Perception* 9, no. 1 (1985): 13–15.

Walker, Alan. "Social Policy and Elderly People in Great Britain: The Construction of Dependent Social and Economic Status in Old Age." In *Old Age and the Welfare State*, edited by Anne-Marie Guillemard, pp. 143–167. Beverly Hills: Sage, 1983.

Walker, Kenneth N.; MacBride, Arlene; and Vachon, Mary L.S. "Social Support Networks and the Crisis of Bereavement." *Social Science and Medicine* 11 (1977): 35–41.

Ward, Russell A. "Informal Networks and Well-Being in Later Life: A Research Agenda." *The Gerontologist* 25, no. 1 (1985): 55–61.

Ward, R.; LaGory, M.; and Sherman, S. "The Relative Importance of Social Ties." *The Gerontologist* 22 — Special Issue (1982): 123.

Watson, J. Allen, and Kivett, Vira R. "Influences on the Life Satisfaction of Older Fathers." *Family Coordinator* 25, no. 4 (1976): 482–488.

Weishaus, Sylvia. "Aging is a Family Affair." In *Aging Parents*, edited by P.K. Ragan, pp. 154–174. Los Angeles: University of Southern California Press, 1979.

Weitzman, Lenore J. *The Divorce Revolution: The Unexpected Social and Economic Consequences for Women and Children in America*. New York: Free Press, 1985.

Wilkins, R., and Adams, O.B. "Health Expectancy in Canada Late 1970's: Demographic, Regional and Social Dimensions." *American Journal of Public Health* 79, no. 9 (1983): 1073–1080.

Wiswell, R. "Relaxation, Exercise and Aging." In *Handbook of Mental Health and Aging*, edited by J. Birren and R. Sloane. Englewood Cliffs, N.J.: Prentice-Hall, 1980.

Wolfson, Michael C. "Status Amid Change — Income Inequality in Canada 1965–1983." *Canadian Statistical Review*, February 1986.

Wong, Shirley; Wong, J.; and Arklie, M. "A Mobile Health Assessment Program for the Elderly." *The Canadian Nurse*, March 1985, pp. 27–31.

Young, D.L.; Scythes, C.A.; Zimmerman, S.A.; and Pennell, M.D. "Nutrition of Canadians 65 Years and Over — A Review." *Canadian Journal of Public Health* 77 (September/October 1986): 363–366.

SUBJECT INDEX

NAME INDEX